The Essential Buyer's Guide

MORGAN
PLUS 4

All models, 1985 to 2019

Your marque expert:
Phil Benfield

VELOCE PUBLISHING
THE PUBLISHER OF FINE AUTOMOTIVE BOOKS

Essential Buyer's Guide Series

Alfa Romeo Alfasud (Metcalfe)
Alfa Romeo Alfetta: all saloon/sedan models 1972 to 1984 & coupé models
 1974 to 1987 (Metcalfe)
Alfa Romeo Giulia GT Coupé (Booker)
Alfa Romeo Giulia Spider (Booker)
Audi TT (Davies)
Audi TT Mk2 2006 to 2014 (Durnan)
Austin-Healey Big Healeys (Trummel)
BMW Boxer Twins (Henshaw)
BMW E30 3 Series 1981 to 1994 (Hosier)
BMW GS (Henshaw)
BMW X5 (Saunders)
BMW Z3 Roadster (Fishwick)
BMW Z4: E85 Roadster and E86 Coupé including M and Alpina 2003 to 2009
 (Smitheram)
BSA 350, 441 & 500 Singles (Henshaw)
BSA 500 & 650 Twins (Henshaw)
BSA Bantam (Henshaw)
Choosing, Using & Maintaining Your Electric Bicycle (Henshaw)
Citroën 2CV (Paxton)
Citroën DS & ID (Heilig)
Cobra Replicas (Ayre)
Corvette C2 Sting Ray 1963-1967 (Falconer)
Datsun 240Z 1969 to 1973 (Newlyn)
DeLorean DMC-12 1981 to 1983 (Williams)
Ducati Bevel Twins (Falloon)
Ducati Desmodue Twins (Falloon)
Ducati Desmoquattro Twins – 851, 888, 916, 996, 998, ST4 1988 to 2004
 (Falloon)
Fiat 500 & 600 (Bobbitt)
Ford Capri (Paxton)
Ford Escort Mk1 & Mk2 (Williamson)
Ford Focus RS/ST 1st Generation (Williamson)
Ford Model A – All Models 1927 to 1931 (Buckley)
Ford Model T – All models 1909 to 1927 (Barker)
Ford Mustang – First Generation 1964 to 1973 (Cook)
Ford Mustang – Fifth Generation (2005-2014) (Cook)
Ford RS Cosworth Sierra & Escort (Williamson)
Harley-Davidson Big Twins (Henshaw)
Hillman Imp (Morgan)
Hinckley Triumph triples & fours 750, 900, 955, 1000, 1050, 1200 – 1991-2009
 (Henshaw)
Honda CBR FireBlade (Henshaw)
Honda CBR600 Hurricane (Henshaw)
Honda SOHC Fours 1969-1984 (Henshaw)
Jaguar E-Type 3.8 & 4.2 litre (Crespin)
Jaguar E-type V12 5.3 litre (Crespin)
Jaguar Mark 1 & 2 (All models including Daimler 2.5-litre V8) 1955 to 1969
 (Thorley)
Jaguar New XK 2005-2014 (Thorley)
Jaguar S-Type – 1999 to 2007 (Thorley)
Jaguar X-Type – 2001 to 2009 (Thorley)
Jaguar XJ-S (Crespin)
Jaguar XJ6, XJ8 & XJR (Thorley)
Jaguar XK 120, 140 & 150 (Thorley)
Jaguar XK8 & XKR (1996-2005) (Thorley)
Jaguar/Daimler XJ 1994-2003 (Crespin)
Jaguar/Daimler XJ40 (Crespin)
Jaguar/Daimler XJ6, XJ12 & Sovereign (Crespin)
Kawasaki Z1 & Z900 (Orritt)
Land Rover Discovery Series 1 (1989-1998) (Taylor)
Land Rover Discovery Series 2 (1998-2004) (Taylor)
Land Rover Series I, II & IIA (Thurman)
Land Rover Series III (Thurman)
Lotus Elan, S1 to Sprint and Plus 2 to Plus 2S 130/5 1962 to 1974 (Vale)
Lotus Europa, S1, S2, Twin-cam & Special 1966 to 1975 (Vale)
Lotus Seven replicas & Caterham 7: 1973-2013 (Hawkins)
Mazda MX-5 Miata (Mk1 1989-97 & Mk2 98-2001) (Crook)
Mazda RX-8 (Parish)
Mercedes-Benz 190: all 190 models (W201 series) 1982 to 1993 (Parish)
Mercedes-Benz 280-560SL & SLC (Bass)

Mercedes-Benz G-Wagen (Greene)
Mercedes-Benz Pagoda 230SL, 250SL & 280SL roadsters & coupés (Bass)
Mercedes-Benz S-Class W126 Series (Zoporowski)
Mercedes-Benz S-Class Second Generation W116 Series (Parish)
Mercedes-Benz SL R129-series 1989 to 2001 (Parish)
Mercedes-Benz SLK (Bass)
Mercedes-Benz W123 (Parish)
Mercedes-Benz W124 – All models 1984-1997 (Zoporowski)
MG Midget & A-H Sprite (Horler)
MG TD, TF & TF1500 (Jones)
MGA 1955-1962 (Crosier)
MGB & MGB GT (Williams)
MGF & MG TF (Hawkins)
Mini (Paxton)
Morgan Plus 4 (Benfield)
Morris Minor & 1000 (Newell)
Moto Guzzi 2-valve big twins (Falloon)
New Mini (Collins)
Norton Commando (Henshaw)
Peugeot 205 GTI (Blackburn)
Piaggio Scooters – all modern two-stroke & four-stroke automatic models
 1991 to 2016 (Willis)
Porsche 356 (Johnson)
Porsche 911 (964) (Streather)
Porsche 911 (991) (Streather)
Porsche 911 (993) (Streather)
Porsche 911 (996) (Streather)
Porsche 911 (997) – Model years 2004 to 2009 (Streather)
Porsche 911 (997) – Second generation models 2009 to 2012 (Streather)
Porsche 911 Carrera 3.2 (Streather)
Porsche 911SC (Streather)
Porsche 924 – All models 1976 to 1988 (Hodgkins)
Porsche 928 (Hemmings)
Porsche 930 Turbo & 911 (930) Turbo (Streather)
Porsche 944 (Higgins)
Porsche 981 Boxster & Cayman (Streather)
Porsche 986 Boxster (Streather)
Porsche 987 Boxster and Cayman 1st generation
 (2005-2009) (Streather)
Porsche 987 Boxster and Cayman 2nd generation (2009-2012) (Streather)
Range Rover – First Generation models 1970 to 1996 (Taylor)
Range Rover – Second Generation 1994-2001 (Taylor)
Range Rover – Third Generation L322 (2002-2012) (Taylor)
Reliant Scimitar GTE (Payne)
Rolls-Royce Silver Shadow & Bentley T-Series (Bobbitt)
Rover 2000, 2200 & 3500 (Marrocco)
Royal Enfield Bullet (Henshaw)
Subaru Impreza (Hobbs)
Sunbeam Alpine (Barker)
Triumph 350 & 500 Twins (Henshaw)
Triumph Bonneville (Henshaw)
Triumph Herald & Vitesse (Ayre)
Triumph Spitfire and GT6 (Ayre)
Triumph Stag (Mort)
Triumph Thunderbird, Trophy & Tiger (Henshaw)
Triumph TR2 & TR3 – All models (including 3A & 3B) 1953 to 1962
 (Conners)
Triumph TR4/4A & TR5/250 - All models 1961 to 1968 (Child & Battyll)
Triumph TR6 (Williams)
Triumph TR7 & TR8 (Williams)
Triumph Trident & BSA Rocket III (Rooke)
TVR Chimaera and Griffith (Kitchen)
TVR S-series (Kitchen)
Velocette 350 & 500 Singles 1946 to 1970 (Henshaw)
Vespa Scooters – Classic 2-stroke models 1960-2008 (Paxton)
Volkswagen Bus (Copping)
Volkswagen Transporter T4 (1990-2003) (Copping/Cservenka)
VW Golf GTI (Copping)
VW Beetle (Copping)
Volvo 700/900 Series (Beavis)
Volvo P1800/1800S, E & ES 1961 to 1973 (Murray)

www.veloce.co.uk

First published in February 2020 by Veloce Publishing Limited, Veloce House, Parkway Farm Business Park, Middle Farm Way, Poundbury, Dorchester DT1 3AR, England. Tel: 01305 260068 / Fax 01305 268864 / e-mail info@veloce.co.uk / web www.veloce.co.uk or www.velocebooks.com.
ISBN 978-1-787115-58-3 / UPC 6-36847-01558-9

A Duratec GDI Plus 4 on the open road.

The Morgan Plus 4 was launched at the Earls Court Motor Show in 1950, following the success of the Morgan 4/4. Since then, the Plus 4 has become a firm favourite with fans of the marque. Although much has been written about the Plus 4 up to 1969, there is little guidance on the car since its relaunch in 1985, particularly cars up to the present day. Whilst much of the information in this guide can be used on the earlier models, I have concentrated on cars from 1985 onward, as there are more of these available on the marketplace.

This book features detailed coverage of the model as it evolved over recent decades, and contains basic considerations prior to purchase, details of running costs, an in-depth guide to what to look for when assessing a potential purchase, and a guide to the common faults that can occur.

Chapter 9's easy-to-use calculator provides a means of working out a car's overall condition by scoring each area being viewed. It will either confirm that the car you are viewing is 'the one,' or will help you to identify potential future areas of expenditure.

An inviting Plus 4 interior.

A later car may fly through the visual inspection, as it should be in good condition, and this would allow you to focus on any extras the car has, and to determine whether it has the right look for you.

The last section gives vital data on the different models since 1985. A full list of options is not provided for each year, though, as this would require a whole separate book. However, the key facts and points are included to help you determine whether a car is genuine.

With my over 28 years' experience in a Morgan main dealership, from mechanic to selling in excess of 100 Morgans per year, I feel confident that this book will benefit you in assessing and purchasing a Plus 4, confirm your choice of model, and set you off on your quintessentially British Morgan journey.

Thanks

A number of people have kindly helped in collating information and providing photographs for this book (their assistance has been invaluable):

Roy Smith for encouraging me to put my knowledge in print, and also for providing a number of photographs.
Brands Hatch Morgan, Melvyn Rutter and Williams Automobiles for the use of a number of their photographs, and for confirming some details.
Additional photographs kindly supplied by Simon Burns and Vanessa Barham.
Morgan Motor Company for the use of its media centre.

A typical club gathering.

Valerie, my wife, for putting up with me writing this book, and for spending hours proofreading it for me.

Original Morgan by John Worrall and Liz Turner (ISBN 9780760316443) is an excellent reference guide and has been a great help on the Fiat and M16 Plus 4s.

Publisher's note

Because of the range of options, engines, gearboxes, construction materials and manufacturing techniques used in the production of this long lived model, the whole book should be read carefully before any vehicle inspection, and points salient to the particular model highlighted.

To help you with the detailed checks outlined in the book, we've added a checklist to chapter 7, and sumarised the points to check in chapter 9 on a single page at the end of that chapter. Both of these pages provide 'at a glance' references to the points you need to check.

Contents

Introduction
– the purpose of this book.. 3

1 Is it the right car for you?
– marriage guidance 7

2 Cost considerations
– affordable, or a money pit? 11

3 Living with a Plus 4
– will you get along together? 13

4 Relative values
– which model for you? 17

5 Before you view
– be well informed 22

6 Inspection equipment
– these items will really help 24

7 Fifteen minute evaluation
– walk away or stay? 26

8 Key points
– where to look for problems 36

9 Serious evaluation
– 60 minutes for years of enjoyment 40

10 Auctions
– sold! Another way to buy your
dream. 69

11 Paperwork
– correct documentation is
essential! 71

12 What's it worth?
– let your head rule your heart 74

13 Do you really want to restore?
– it'll take longer and cost more
than you think. 78

14 Paint problems
– bad complexion, including
dimples, pimples and bubbles 80

15 Problems due to lack of use
– just like their owners, Plus 4s
need exercise! 83

16 The Community
– key people, organisations and
companies in the Plus 4 world 86

17 Vital statistics
– essential data at your fingertips .. 89

Index 95

Notes 96

The Essential Buyer's Guide™ currency

At the time of publication a BG unit of currency "●" equals approximately £1.00/US$1.32/Euro 1.18. Please adjust to suit current exchange rates using Sterling as the base currency.

Front view of a Plus 4 two-seater.

Tall and short drivers

Whether you're 5ft or 6ft 3in you should be able to fit in and drive a Morgan. There are two considerations for the taller driver, though: check that the hood clears your head (four-seaters have increased headroom); and, if you have an inside leg measurement of 33in or less you will be fine, otherwise you may prefer a 14in steering wheel for comfort, and to give clearance when changing gears. Rear legroom is limited on the four-seater, and is better suited to accommodating children or luggage, especially if the driver is tall.

Controls

All factory-built Plus 4s are fitted with manual gearboxes.

Generally speaking there's no power steering, and servo-assisted brakes became standard only in 1992.

Power steering on Plus 4s did not become an option until 2014, and was taken off the option list in

Five-speed gearbox.

Latest GDI instruments.

November 2016. However, aftermarket systems are available if you feel the steering is too heavy. Most buyers are pleasantly surprised by the feel and feedback of the standard steering setup.

Will it fit in your garage?
Bumpers, overriders and variations in wheel size can result in slight differences in the dimensions of individual vehicles. For the purposes of this guide, though, maximum sizes have been used. Plus 4s are 13ft long by 5ft 4in wide (3980mm by 1640mm). Allow an extra 8in (203mm) in length if the car is a four-seater fitted with a luggage rack.

Usability
Classic 1930s looks with modern running gear. Although not normally used every day they are certainly up to the job. Four-seaters are slightly more practical, offering some rear space (for children or extra luggage). A luggage rack allows for an increase in luggage capacity. Two-seater models have a cleaner roof line, compared to a four-seater, but with the roof down they both look good. An ideal 'classic,' where you can turn the key and just go.

Parts availability
Excellent. Most parts are still available from the Morgan factory via the dealer network, and there are many specialists providing upgrades and some of the more obscure/older items.

Two-seater luggage rack with sidescreen storage.

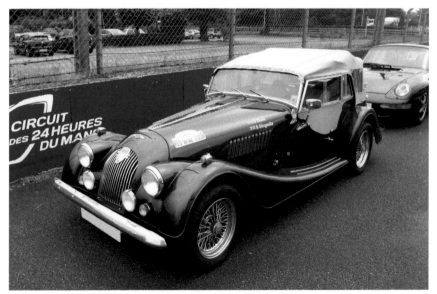

Plus 4 long-door T16 four-seater model. An extremely rare car as these were only produced in 1998.

Front overrider available from 2004, instead of bumpers. Both options are popular.

Insurance
Even a new example can be insured on a classic car policy. Most buyers pay between ●x175-350 a year on a limited mileage policy. Agreed values can be arranged with various specialist companies, and are recommended.

Running costs
Remarkably low for such a specialised car. Standard models will easily achieve good fuel economy with miles per gallon in the mid-30s to low-40s being achievable. Low insurance costs and good reliability mean a Morgan does not hit the pocket like some other classic sports cars.

Prices and investment potential
Morgans are well known for holding their value, though one should always expect some depreciation. However, the longer you keep the car the more the depreciation will be spread out. The value may well increase over time, but treat this as a potential bonus. You can at least expect to get the bulk of the purchase price back on resale if you keep the car in good condition. Joy of ownership, touring, and entering the Morgan lifestyle should be the reasons for purchase, rather than as an investment.

Alternatives
There isn't really a direct alternative. Classic sports cars from the 1950s and 1960s may be considered for their character, or modern, mass-produced sports cars with the latest engines and running gear. The Morgan is nicely placed with old world charm and character, but with modern, reliable running gear, so you do not have to be mechanically minded or have to tinker.

2 Cost considerations
– affordable, or a money pit?

Servicing is recommended every 5000 miles/12 months. Latest handbooks say 10,000-mile/12-month intervals but most owners struggle to complete anywhere near this mileage over 12 months.

Timing belts are fitted on Fiat, Rover M16 and T16 engines: they should be changed every five years or 60,000 miles. The Ford Duratec engines used in later models are chain driven.

Servicing costs
Medium/5000-mile service.. .. .. ●x433
Full service/10,000 miles .. .. ●x570
Timing belt change (M16/T16) .. .. ●x218

Mechanical parts
Brake pads and discs. .. .. ●x234
Rear wheel cylinders pre-1992 .. .. ●x50
Rear wheel cylinders 1992-on .. .. ●x97
Clutch master cylinder (M16/T16 models) .. .. ●x182
Clutch slave cylinder .. .. ●x132
Standard kingpin .. .. ●x44
Kingpin bush (two required per side) .. .. ●x19
Rear leaf spring .. .. ●x206
Front main spring .. .. ●x31
Radiator refurbishment .. .. ●x216
Upgraded aluminium radiator.. .. .. ●x696
Trackrod end .. .. ●x45
Steering rack gaiter .. .. ●x83
Handbrake cable .. .. ●x101

Bodywork parts
Front wing 'Superform' aluminium .. .. ●x1376
Rear wing 'Superform' aluminium .. .. ●x637
Overrider (2003-on) .. .. ●x260
Stainless steel bumper (1998-on) with end caps. .. .. ●x637
Windscreen glass up to 1998 . .. . ●x228
Heated windscreen assembly . .. . ●x925
Windscreen wiper blade . .. . ●x13
Door mirror. .. .. ●x58
Painted wire wheel.. .. .. ●x226
Original quality tyre 195/60x15 .. .. ●x65
Galvanised chassis . .. . ●x2010
Valance (stainless steel) .. .. ●x504

Electrical items
Headlamp (pair) .. .. ●x74
Indicator lamp. .. .. ●x26

Indicator stalk (to late-1997) x84
ECU refurbishment x300
Dashboard instrument circuit board (2004-2007) x517
Ignition switch assembly. x136
Fuel-injection relay x10

Trim and restoration (examples)
New hood PVC two-seater. x935
New hood mohair four-seater x1320
Full interior re-trim in leather x4235
New carpet set x575
Full bare metal repaint x6000

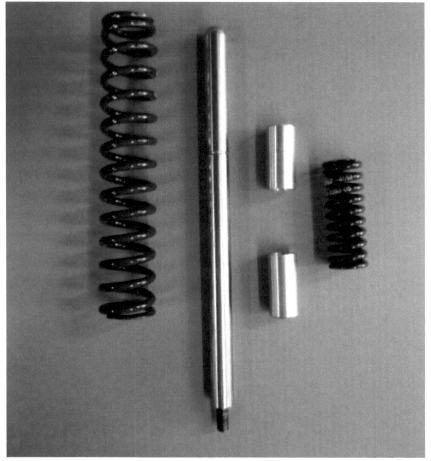

Typical parts required for a kingpin overhaul. Stub axle bushes will need reaming out once fitted.

3 Living with a Plus 4

– will you get along together?

There are a number of things you must decide before buying a Morgan Plus 4. You must ask yourself the following questions (honest answers will enable you to choose the ideal model to suit your needs):

A blast in the country. Plus 4 Works Editions enjoying the Malvern hills.

What are you going to use the car for?
Local runs, car shows and country lanes, weekends away, regular commuting, higher mileage touring holidays? If the answer is the latter, you may prefer a newer model. If you fancy the odd track day or fast club runs to Le Mans, however, a tuned model may be better suited.

Do you have children or need extra luggage capacity?
If yes, then you may prefer a four-seater. Consider the age of your children and whether they are interested in going out in a Morgan; children older than early teens, and taller individuals generally, may find the rear seats a bit cramped. You may find in reality the two-seater is the better bet.

What do you drive now?
Are you used to a larger engine, eg 3.0-litre or above? Is a 2.0-litre engine going to feel underpowered? Does it have enough torque compared to what you are used to? Try to think of yourself after three months of ownership. Do you think you are going to want to extract more power from the car, or fit performance upgrades? If

Interior on a later 2006 four-seater: ideal for children, small dogs or extra luggage.

Bonnet louvres are individually hand-pressed. The view is timeless, and part of a Morgan's special character.

This car has HillsAlive fitted luggage on the rear shelf.

so, a Roadster or a Plus 8 may be the better choice, and would work out cheaper in the long run.

What mileage are you likely to cover?

Most owners do half of what they expect to cover during a 12-month period; so 2500 miles per year is quite common. Unfortunately, work, life and other pressures can sometimes take over and your Morgan then gets left in the garage. This may assist when buying insurance as you may be able to reduce the cost by putting the car on a limited mileage policy. However, lack of use is probably the main reason for cars coming up for sale.

Morgans have evolved over the years, so a 1990 M16 Plus 4 will feel quite different to a 2016 example. The newer cars will feel more modern and lighter to drive. The difference is even greater when compared to a 1951 flat-rad example. Hence, I have avoided going back to the pre-1969 models in this guide.

Every Morgan is different. You have a choice of 50,000 colours, over 30 leathers, and a long options list, so no two cars are ever the same. Because they are hand-made, they all feel very slightly different, even when compared to another example built on the same day. This is the soul of the car, and very few manufacturers or models have it. This is what you're buying in to. You can't put your finger on what it is, but once you feel it you are hooked.

So, despite its foibles, a Morgan Plus 4 will get under your skin, become part of the family, and could even be given a name.

Once you have the car you become part of an extended family. The Morgan Sports Car Club (MSCC) is huge, with local groups and regular events. Other owners, enthusiasts, and the public at large love the cars, and you will rarely hear of any vandalism, or attempted theft; you can leave your car almost anywhere and people will come up to talk to you and admire it. At some point in your ownership you may decide to do a factory tour. You can see the build process and talk to the people who made your car. The experience is priceless.

If you want all the latest electronic driver aids, touch screens, climate control and top quality sound systems, then a Morgan Plus 4 probably isn't for you. If you want adventure, feel and feedback through the steering, loads of character, and a heap of fun within the speed limits, then you will easily learn to live with the Plus 4.

Yes, the fly-off handbrake takes a little getting used to. There is nowhere to put your clutch foot (you'll soon learn to rest it lightly on the pedal); clutches rarely wear out before you ask. Alternatively, you'll adjust the position of your foot so It is between the clutch and the brake pedals; after a while you will do it without thinking.

Getting in and out gracefully, especially with the hood up, takes a bit of practice. The interior is cosy, and the seats are comfortable, even the fixed-backed ones. Expect the odd drip when it rains – it *is* a convertible.

So, if you think you'll get along with a Plus 4, begin by pinning down the age range of the model, then the budget you want to spend, and let the fun begin!

Out on the road or a club meeting, any excuse to use a Plus 4.

4 Relative values
– which model for you?

This chapter shows in percentage terms the relative value of each model produced since 1985. Every Morgan is different, and value here assumes a car in good condition, with low mileage and a range of common extras. The value percenages expressed are in relation to the Plus 4 110 Edition at 100%.

Plus 4 Fiat
Two-seater **40%**
Four-seater **40%**

1985 Fiat-engined four-seater.

Plus 4 Rover M16 1987-1992
Two-seater **50%**
Four-seater **50%**

Early Rover-engined Plus 4.

Plus 4 Rover T16 1992-1997 Short-door models
Two-seater **65%**
Four-seater **60%**

Plus 4 T16 four-seater.

Plus 4 Rover T16 1998-2000 Long-door models
Two-seater **75%**
Four-seater **75%** (these are very rare as they were only made in 1998)

Ford Duratec Plus 4.

Plus 4 Ford Duratec and GDI

Two-seater **90-100%**
Four-seater **70%** (built between 2006–2016)
Sport models identified with black wire wheels and no spare wheel **75%**

Plus 4 Super Sport
130%

Plus 4 Babydoll
140% (only 15 produced to mid-2019)

Plus 4 Super Sport, one of only three in Primrose Yellow.

Plus 4 Babydoll.

ARP4 in Metallic Prosecco.

Plus 4 110 Edition.

Plus 4 Works Edition.

A rare Duratec Plus 4 with a narrow body. Only one GDI narrow body was produced.

Plus 4 ARP4
130%

Plus 4 110 Edition
100%

Plus 4 Works Edition
120%

5 Before you view
– be well informed

To avoid a wasted journey, and the disappointment of finding that the car doesn't
match your expectations, it will help if you're very clear about what questions you
want to ask before you pick up the telephone. Some of these points might appear
basic, but, when you're excited about the prospect of buying your dream classic,
it's amazing how some of the most obvious things slip the mind ... Also check the
current values of the model you're considering in classic car magazines, which may
give both a price guide and auction results.

Where is the car?
Is it going to be worth travelling to the next county/state, or even across a border?
A locally advertised car, although it may not sound very interesting, can add to your
knowledge for very little effort, so make a visit – it might even be in better condition
than expected.

Dealer or private sale?
Establish early on if the car is being sold by its owner or by a trader. A private
owner should have all the history, so don't be afraid to ask detailed questions. A
dealer may have more limited knowledge of a car's history, but should have some
documentation. A dealer may offer a warranty/guarantee (ask for a printed copy)
and finance.

Cost of collection and delivery?
A dealer may well be used to quoting for delivery by car transporter. A private owner
may agree to meet you halfway, but only agree to this after you've viewed the car at
the vendor's address to validate the documents.

View – when and where?
It's always preferable to view at the vendor's home or business premises. In the case
of a private sale, the car's documentation should tally with the vendor's name and
address. Arrange to view only in daylight, and avoid a damp day (most cars look
better in poor light or when wet).

Reason for sale?
Do make this one of the first questions. Why is the car being sold and how long has
it been with the current owner? How many previous owners?

Left-hand drive to right-hand drive/specials and convertibles
If a steering conversion has been done it can only reduce the value. Furthermore,
it may well be that other aspects of the car still reflect the specification for a foreign
market.

Condition (body/chassis/interior/mechanicals)
Ask for an honest appraisal of the car's condition. Ask specifically about some of the
items/issues described in chapter 7.

All original specification
An original equipment car is invariably of higher value than a customised version.

Matching data/legal ownership
Do VIN/chassis, engine numbers and licence plate match the registration document? Is the owner's name and address recorded in the official document?

For those countries that require an annual test of roadworthiness, does the car have a document showing it complies (an MOT certificate in the UK, which can be verified online or 0845 600 5977)?

If a smog/emissions certificate is mandatory, does the car have one?

If required, does the car carry a current road fund license/licence plate tag?

Does the vendor own the car outright? Money might be owed to a finance company or bank: the car could even be stolen. Several organisations will supply the data on ownership, based on the car's licence plate number, for a fee. Such companies can often also tell you whether the car has been 'written-off' by an insurance company. In the UK these organisations* can supply vehicle data:

DVLA	0844 453 0118	HPI	0113 222 2010
AA	0800 056 8040	RAC	0330 159 0364

Unleaded fuel (irrelevant?)
If necessary, has the car been modified to run on unleaded fuel?

Insurance
Check with your existing insurer before setting out, your current policy might not cover you to drive the car if you do purchase it.

How you can pay
A cheque/check will take several days to clear and the seller may prefer to sell to a cash buyer. However, a banker's draft (a cheque issued by a bank) is a good as cash, but safer, so contact your own bank and become familiar with the formalities that are necessary to obtain one.

Buying at auction?
If the intention is to buy at auction see chapter 10 for further advice.

Professional vehicle check (mechanical examination)
There are often marque/model specialists who will undertake professional examination of a vehicle on your behalf. Owners clubs will be able to put you in touch with such specialists.

Other organisations* that will carry out a general professional check in the UK are:

AA	0800 056 8040 / www.theaa.com/vehicle-inspection (motoring organisation with vehicle inspectors)
RAC	0330 159 0720 / www.rac.co.uk/buying-a-car/vehicle-inspections; (motoring organisation with vehicle inspectors)

*Other countries will have similar organisations.

6 Inspection equipment
– these items will really help

This book
Reading glasses (if you need them for close work)
Magnet (fridge magnet is ideal)
Torch (flashlight or mobile phone light)
Probe (a small screwdriver)
Overalls and a cushion/pillow
Mirror on a stick
Digital camera
A friend, preferably a knowledgeable enthusiast

Go prepared, remember to bring the list of questions you prepared earlier, and definitely take the following items:

This book
This book is designed to be your guide, so take it along and use the check boxes in chapter 9 to help you assess each area of the car you're interested in. Don't be afraid to let the seller see you using it.

Reading glasses (if you need them for close work)
For checking paperwork and close inspections, you would be amazed by how many people forget to take them.

Magnet (fridge magnet is ideal)
Wrap in a thin soft cloth and gain permission before using it on the body panels. Most later cars will have aluminium panels (magnets won't stick to aluminium panels).

Wings could be steel or aluminium up until 1998, aluminium from 1998. Aftermarket fibreglass wings are available and may have been fitted during accident repairs or restoration. Some filler around the headlamps on both types of wings is to be expected. At least you will know what type of panels are fitted.

Torch (flashlight or mobile phone light)
Ideal for checking those dark areas of the engine bay, underneath and inside the car. Ensure it has fresh batteries or is fully charged.

Probe (a small screwdriver)
Use finger pressure to check and only use the probe if something needs further examination. Agree with the vendor first before using it, and explain why you wish to check a certain area.

Overalls and a cushion/pillow
You will get dirty when checking the underside and mechanical parts. Wear disposable gloves or ensure you wash your hands before touching any of the interior, paintwork or weather equipment. Use the cushion to kneel on when checking in the footwells and underside.

Mirror on a stick
Handy to view those 'hard to see' areas, particularly when used together with a torch.

Digital camera or smartphone
Take pictures for later reference or if you require a second opinion on an area of concern.

A friend, preferably a knowledgeable enthusiast
Ideally have a friend or knowledgeable enthusiast accompany you – a second opinion is always valuable.

7 Fifteen minute evaluation
– walk away or stay?

Be objective. It's easy for your heart to rule your head when viewing a car. Remember, too, that 'All that glitters is not gold.' Despite the value of a Plus 4, you're still looking at a used car, which may be older than it appears, and is unlikely to be in as-new condition.

Exterior

Walk around the car, starting at one of the front corners, and record any noticeable damage to the bodywork (dents, larger stone chips, paint condition, and any corrosion, particularly on the wing edges). Being hand-made, tolerances can vary, but they should be consistent. Do the bonnets and doors fit well? Is there a gap on the bonnet centre strip to the brass hinge ends? If so, this indicates the cowl may have been removed at some point (ask why). Doors rubbing at the bottom of the screen deck and elbow panel is common, particularly on older cars.

Bonnet centre strip hinge gap highlights if the cowl and bonnets have been removed. This one needs realigning.

Open the bonnets (rear catch first and then the front one to open, front then rear to close: you'll soon learn the technique). Bonnet straps should not have to hold down the bonnets, they are for decoration only. Wings should fit neatly up to the bulkhead, with neat screws or Allen key heads, not misaligned large bolts. Bonnets should not have rubbed onto the tops of the wings. If they have, you're looking at a fair amount of time and expense to put this right, or it can be a sign of something far more sinister (such as a poorly-executed rebuild).

There should be a join between the screen deck and the elbow panel about halfway along the door. The elbow panels can crack slightly further back; this can be just a stress crack from the panel fitting screws/tacks caused by time and use, or a sign

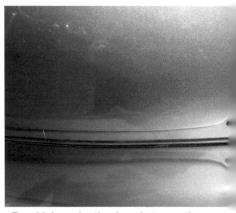

Panel join under the door, between the screen deck and elbow panel.

of deterioration of the wood frame. Make a note to check in more detail if any cracks are found.

Check the lower corners of the rear panel for impact marks. If bumpers are fitted are they straight? It's easy for the bumper to have been nudged, causing the sweep and mounting bolt to flex on impact, thus puncturing the rear panel, and springing back into the original position. The panel can be repaired, though a lot of owners do not spot this kind of damage.

Once you have finished examining the bodywork, stand back and check that the car is sitting level. View from different angles to see if the car lists to one side. Rear springs can sag and kingpins can stick, causing the car to be lower on a particular corner.

Check the windscreen for damage (heated screens from 1998 are expensive to replace). Any of the

Stainless wire wheels are a different colour, with a hint of yellow compared to chrome. Look at the wheel nut on this example.

windscreens can de-laminate from the lower corners. Cracks from the mounting screws on the side of the screen could be caused by a hood that has shrunk.

Once an exterior body examination has been carried out, check the wheels and tyres. Tyres are date stamped, and, despite a good tread depth, should be checked for age-related cracks. If they are over ten years old they will definitely need to be changed, regardless of condition.

Note the appearance of wire wheels. It's cheaper to replace a very rusty chrome wire wheel than to have it re-chromed. Stainless wire wheels became an option from 2003, and have a similar appearance to chrome. Stainless wheels have a slight yellow finish compared to the wheel nut or eared spinner, if fitted. Grey-painted wire wheels have been the standard fit from 1985 to date. Plus 8 alloy wheels have been available as an option from late 2004. It's not simple to convert from alloys to wires as the wing fitment is different. Black wire wheels were added to the options list in 2010, and Roadster 16in wires have been a cost option since 2012.

Underside and bulkhead

Examine the underside, bulkhead and valances (inner wings) next. The bulkhead and valances were undersealed until 1986. On cars produced between 1986 and 1998 these were powder-coated and undersealed. This coincides with 'wings off' paintwork becoming officially standard. From 1998 the bulkhead and valances became stainless.

On the driver's side at the point the steering shaft is mounted and goes through the valance, the panel is double-skinned. The panel can corrode at the points noted above, as well as along the lower section and at the rear by the bulkhead. The valances can be changed with the front wing in situ, but allow eight to ten hours per side.

Bulkheads can rot where the valances bolt onto them, where the bulkhead mounts into the chassis, and where the toolbox is mounted on the earlier cars, but can be repaired if the top of the bulkhead is in good order. It's very common for the

Extremely rusty bulkhead, heater box removed. This one is beyond repair.

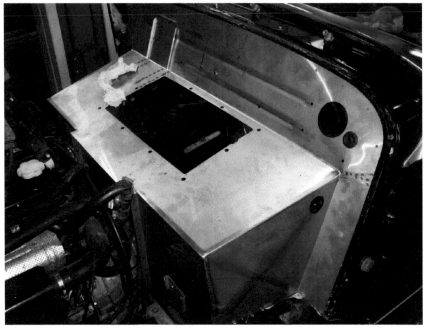

Stainless bulkheads were introduced in 1998, and can now be fitted to earlier cars during restoration or accident repair.

bulkheads to have been repainted or treated with Hammerite on 1986-1998 cars. If the bulkhead powder-coating is in good original condition, it's a helpful sign of how the car has been kept.

Chassis

A galvanised chassis has been an option since 1986, and became standard in 1998. A steel chassis with an Autophoetic coating has been fitted since December 2015. Check early steel chassis for rust in the following places: under the triangle plates by the front crossmembers; along the chassis rails where the floorboards are mounted; lever arm rear shock absorber mountings; and the rear crossmember. Visually check all the crossmembers. Galvanised chassis can crack, particularly in the engine bay area, so do not assume that just because it's galvanised it will be fine. Don't be put off by a car with a non-galvanised chassis. If the chassis is in good condition it will last for years. I have known 40-year-old cars whose original chassis is in excellent condition.

You can see the bulk of the chassis from inside the engine bay and from the underside of the car. Check the chassis number is present: it's stamped behind the driver's seat on the crossmember on earlier cars, and on the crossmember in front of the driver's seat on cars from 1998. Later cars will have a 17-digit chassis number.

Check the chassis for damage and for ripples along the sides and flat sections. Although it's of a relatively simple ladder-type construction, there's a limit to what can be straightened. Frontal damage impact force will travel down the length of the car, and may cause ripples in the chassis by the axle; check this carefully if the car has been classified as an insurance total loss and then rebuilt.

Wood frame

Morgan cars have never had a wooden chassis. They have a wooden body frame mounted onto the metal chassis. The body frame is constructed of ash and then panelled in steel or aluminium. The wood frames have been treated with Cuprinol since 1986 as standard; some earlier cars are known to have been treated from 1984. Other than the Fiat models, all of the later cars will have a treated wood frame. It is rare to have wood issues on these later cars, but you still need to check the frame.

Open the doors and check for play: a little play in the door hinges is normal, particularly on the driver's side. Also check that the hinge post doesn't move at the bottom. Check the tacks on the threshold strips: if any are missing or coming adrift this could be a sign that the rocker has gone soft. You can check the rocker by feeling (carefully) with your finger and thumb along the inside, under the draught excluder. You should feel the edge of the wood along the top and side as you work from the front to the back. The rear sections can rot, in which case you will suddenly find that the edge will disappear. You can check this using only finger pressure, without doing any damage to the interior trim. With the door still open, and with light pressure, hold the top of the elbow rail and see if there is any play or movement in the bottom joint. Definitely check this area if there is a split starting to form in the elbow panel.

Check under the front wing where it mounts on the sill board. Light pressure can be applied to check the condition of the wood.

Examine inside the rear wheelarches, particularly in the corners, and the rear frame at the point where the back panel mounts on to it. The rear frame is

Sillboard and rocker sections of the wood frame.

commonly referred to the 'rear goal post,' and the joints can deteriorate. It's more accessible on four-seaters.

If the Plus 4 has bumpers, examine the numberplate panel. If it's loose check that the mounting screws are secure and that the wood behind the panel is sound. Morgan had a period, from 2004-2006, where a clear underseal wax treatment was used – the appearance of the wood can be a little alarming as it looks untreated.

Interior

Vinyl, also known as Ambla, was standard fitment until September 2008, with leather being a cost option. The leather range used was originally Connolly HB pack or the Autolux ranges. This was changed to Muirhead and Yarwood ranges on later cars. Since 2008, black or tan leather has been standard; other colours were and remain a cost option. It is extremely difficult to obtain HB style leathers with the antique-looking grain now, due to current tanning techniques. Extreme waterproof leather has been an additional option since 2014.

Check the condition of the leather. If it's saggy on the sill boards, double-check the wood, as the padding may have become soaked causing wet rot. Water staining on the leather on the sills is quite common on cars that have been used in all weathers. Any water that comes in accumulates on the sills, especially if the sidescreens have not been tucked into the hood properly.

Wear on the driver's seat edge and on the elbow panel edge is to be expected. Elbow rail protectors can be purchased to improve this area.

Rover M16 engine bay: note replacement heater box foam and incorrect wing mounting washers. Penny washers are never fitted on the top of the wings.

Walnut dashboards look fantastic, but can bleach and crack due to age and sunlight damage.

Bright-coloured leathers show more wear than darker shades, even on very low mileage cars.

The driver's seat base webbing can collapse. This may be the case if the seat cushion looks very flat, or if you feel as if you're sitting in the frame rather than on the seat. Headrests were optional until 1998.

Walnut dashboards have always been an optional extra and remain so to date. They can bleach and crack in strong sunlight. Carpets can also bleach in the sun, and can become bald in places due to wear, damp or moth damage, particularly under the seats. On two-seater models you can lift out the rear board behind the seats; a great way of looking at the rear suspension or to see if the tool tray is intact (as fitted on post-2004 cars).

Weather equipment

The earlier, studded, windscreen hoods take a little practice to put up. Once you've mastered the technique, though, it will take approximately two minutes. Later hoods, introduced in 2003, are easier to fit, and can be lowered more quickly. You can also release the rear of the later hood to gain access to the luggage area.

Up until 2000, Plus 4 two-seaters would have originally been supplied with a black vinyl, studded-type roof, outer sidescreens, and a tonneau. This earlier style of hood has been an option since 2004. Coloured PVC/vinyl and mohair were cost options. Plus 4 four-seaters up to 1998 were also supplied with rear sidescreens and a hood frame cover. From 2004 the car has been fitted with the new, easier fitting, Morgan '20-second hood' in black vinyl, and with sidescreens. A tonneau cover, coloured PVC and mohair are optional.

On the latest cars weather equipment is available in coloured PVC or mohair as options. In addition to the hood itself the choice is for either a hood frame cover and sidescreen bag or a tonneau and sidescreen bag. The four-seaters from 2006 had similar packages. Customers quite often have additional weather equipment made from a mix of the available materials, for example PVC hood and a mohair hood frame cover. The main thing is there should be weather equipment with the car. If it is there, check that it all fits and has all its fixings.

There's a technique for putting up the hood (both styles), and the vendor should know how to do this (if not there are a number of videos available online). Aftermarket easier-fitting hoods are available for the earlier style models, and can be desirable on a used car for sale.

Hood condition is important. Hoods aren't off-the-shelf items, but are made to fit individual cars. There are pros and cons on both types of material: vinyl/PVC can shrink with age, discolour (this is particularly noticeable with those in the stone colour), and become stiff in cold weather. However, it is easier to clean than mohair and cheaper to replace. Mohair can get baggy, blister with age, fade, and show wear marks on the 2004-on cars due to how the hood is folded. Mohair has a more attractive appearance, though, which is why it's often chosen.

Tonneau zips can break.

Mechanicals and electrics

Check the following items under the bonnet: fluid levels, hose condition, wiring for evidence of repair or rodent damage, and heater foams. Check inside the toolbox, if fitted, to ensure all items are present, and for signs of any rodent damage. From the mid 1980s to early 1990s a vacuum-formed heater foam was fitted on the heater

Two-seater factory 20-second hood has a very smooth line.

1986-1997 instruments are prone to misting up; switches are very reliable.

box, this disintegrates with age, and has been unavailable for at least 20 years. If it's in good condition it can indicate that the car has had a sheltered life.

Start the car
Does it crank over okay on the starter motor? Are there any strange noises or leaks from the cooling system or engine? With the engine running look underneath to see if there are any fluids dripping. While the car is warming up check that the electrics work.

The newer the car the less chance there is of oil leaks or oil misting on engine surfaces. Heavy oxidisation of the engine bay components can indicate the car has spent a lot of time outside or been used in all weathers. By now you should have a feel as to whether to continue your inspection or to make your excuses and leave.

Fiat engines can leak from the rocker cover gaskets, seals and sump gasket. Rover M16/T16 rocker cover gaskets are prone to leaking, M16 head gaskets can leak from the gallery plug seal area by the back of the cylinder head – this is near to the exhaust outlet by the rearmost cylinder. Check the timing belt covers for wet patches, as this can indicate leakage from the camshaft seals. The oil gauge pipes/unions can also leak.

Listen for exhaust blowing from the manifold areas. Manifold gaskets are prone to leaking on all models up to Duratec.

Ford Duratec engines tend to be leak-free, although sump gaskets can sometimes leak towards the near of the engine.

If all's good so far, then it's time for a more detailed inspection, paying extra attention to any areas where you have noted concerns.

A clean dry Duratec engine.

Vehicle area	✓
Bodywork damage (dents, stone chips, etc)	
Door, bonnet and panel gaps (consistent?)	
Elbow panel condition (any cracks?)	
Impact damage in lower corners?	
Bumpers straight?	
Does the car sit level (any sign of spring sagging?)	
Windscreen condition (damage, de-lamination?)	
Tyre condition/age	
Wheel condition	
Underside, bulkhead and valance condition (powder-coating, underseal, Hammerite condition)	
Chassis condition (steel, galvanised?). Rust or impact damage?	
Wood frame condition	
Interior condition (carpets, vinyl, leather, dashboard)	
Weather equipment fit and condition (hood, sidescreens, tonneau)	
Underbonnet: fluid levels, hose condition, wiring, leaks, exhaust	
Notes	

Weather equipment

Check that all the weather equipment is present and that it fits. Replacements should ideally be made for the specific car to ensure a good fit. Does the tonneau zip close fully when the tonneau is fitted? Wiggle and lift out the headrests to check the condition of the seat leather.

Standard studded windscreen hood fitted until 2000.

Two-seater sidescreen.

Radiators

Morgan radiators, be they brass, aluminium or a plastic combination, can leak. This usually occurs around the top and bottom necks or from the main core. Aftermarket aluminium radiators with a larger capacity core are popular and rarely leak, but should still be checked.

Leaking radiators are common.

Wood frame

Check the following: movement in door hinge posts, sill boards, missing or loose threshold strip tacks. Elbow panels can crack – a possible sign of a weak lower joint.

Interior condition

Leather can wear, particularly on the seats, and can shrink on the sill board areas. Seat base webbing can collapse. Carpets fade.

Wings and general paint condition

Wings can corrode around the edges. Look for bubbling and evidence of repair. Check for evidence of accident repair or poorly-executed paint repairs.

Valance condition

Valances pre-1998 can corrode badly. Carefully check the one on the driver's side, as this is structural for the UK MOT.

Rocker and sillboard.

Early 'tombstone' folding reclining seat.

Aluminium wing showing corrosion.

This driver's side valance is in very poor condition; the bulkhead is also likely to be corroded.

9 Serious evaluation
– 60 minutes for years of enjoyment

Score each section using the boxes as follows:
4 = Excellent; 3 = good; 2 average; 1 poor. The totting up procedure is detailed at the end of the chapter. Be realistic in your marking!

Paint

Since 2012 Morgan paint codes have been stamped on the chassis plate mounted on the bulkhead. Prior to this date, the only record of colour will be on the original sales invoice or in the Morgan factory records.

Check the quality of the paintwork on each panel – is the finish even? Does the colour match the surrounding panels – due to the angles and position of adjacent panels they can appear to be different colours. You are basically checking for consistency. Ask the seller if any panels have been repainted. It's quite common for paintwork to have been carried out, even after only a few years. Look out for localised repairs

Chassis plate with paint code.

on the wings (they are expensive to paint due to the amount of work required for a good finsh). You can usually see an edge, like a tide line, on localised repairs. See also chapter 14, Paint problems.

Body tub panels and rear wings

Examine the body tub in detail, particularly on older cars. Panel fit should be good. Start at the front on one side and make your way around the car. Door handles were an option until 1997, whereupon they became a standard fitment. The doors can rub slightly at the bottom (inner skin against the lower screen deck section and elbow panel). Open the door and check for rubbing at these points. The top rear corner of the door can rub against the elbow panel, causing a little worn triangle. The bodies do flex, so some wear will occur with use. Is this wear consistent with the mileage and age of the car? Pre-1998 cars can have steel door skins; check with a magnet if you're unsure. The outer door skins can bubble towards the bottom. If the sidescreens are fitted, remove them and check the paintwork around the sidescreen mounting bracket: paintwork can bubble from around the screw holes. Screen decks were steel up until 2002. Check that the door hinge beading strip is in place.

Examine the lower section of the screen deck and elbow panel where it joins the wing beading: rust can bubble up along this area. Have a close look at the wing and around the wing treads for rust bubbling and localised repairs.

Carrying on over the elbow panel there is a joint at the rear where it meets the rear quarter panel on four-seaters or the back panel on two-seaters. Look carefully for paint repairs at the top of the panels, and for any overspray on the interior trim

Light corrosion by wing beading.

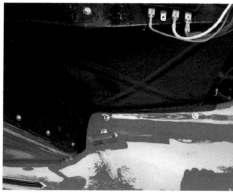

Cutting-in of the wings is an important area of detail.

Seam between elbow panel and rear panel.

1995 wing fitment. Note the mounting screws.

Rear stainless bumper with end caps, mounting bolt can damage the back panel on minor impacts.

2019 wing fitment. Allen key screws are used on later cars.

edges. Examine the rear panels, and, if bumpers are fitted, re-check for impact damage: it's easy to miss. Numberplate mounting panels can corrode around the edges. Check that the panel is not loose. Wing beading fit should be tight between the panels.

Examine the rear wings. Look at each wing at the 12 o'clock position, and note how many fingers you can get between the wing edge and outer edge of the tyre: the gap should be consistent on both sides. Check the wing edge for corrosion, chips on the front face, and dents in the wing where people have leaned on them when getting in and out. Check the 10mm beading edge on the wing when looking square-on to the wheel between the 10 and 11 o'clock positions. Check for cracked paint and for a bulge in the wing, when viewed from the rear to the front of the car. It's very common for the rear wings to be nudged on the rear corners (the wing then bows out and can crack the paint at this beading point). A minor kink can be pulled back straight; more serious damage may require that the wing be professionally reshaped and repainted. Check at the bottom of the rear wing beading for corrosion and for scrape damage.

Make your way around to the other side of the car and carry out the same checks, comparing your finger test results with the previous side.

Stand back from the car and check the ride height by looking at the gap from the top of each rear tyre to the bottom of the wing at the 12 o'clock position. Any differences may indicate suspension issues. Up to an inch (25mm) is within manufacturing tolerances.

Once you have finished assessing the tub move on to checking the front wings in detail.

Front wings, bonnets and cowl

Examine the front wings carefully for panel fit, paint finish and for corrosion. Pre-1998 wings are non-superform, and are constructed in five sections, so can corrode partway down the vertical side, as well as around the edges. All pre-1998 wings have a ¾in (19mm) lip running down most of their length, and stays are attached to this area. Later, post-1998 cars do not have the lip, and the wing stay support is bonded on. The 10mm bead edge running around the base of the wing is also bonded on, and a number of early wings of this style can suffer paint bubbling due to a reaction with the bonding agent.

Aluminium wings up to 1998 have a steel rod fitted around the inside of the wing – the aluminium is wrapped around it at the edge. Water can enter this area and an electrolytic reaction can occur, corroding the wing edge and exposing the rod. This is costly to put right, so a new wing may be an easier and cheaper solution. Steel wings can also corrode in the same place, though it's easier to carry out weld repairs.

Other points to note: paint can crack around the headlamps; there's less filler applied to the superform wings, and cars with sidelights mounted on the wings (standard fit until August 2008) have a bracket underneath with a thin rubber pad – this sidelight bolt hole can corrode and the bracket may eventually wear a hole in the wing. This area can be repaired by welding in a new section.

Bonnet and cowl should fit well. There should be an even gap around the screen deck area, with no noticeable gap between the chrome strip and bonnet brass ends.

Check the cowl for impact damage from behind, it may have been dented

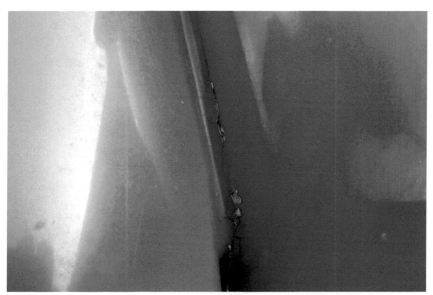

Front wing showing a crack in the filler around the headlamp pod.
This is very common.

Sidelights on the tops of the wings were standard fit until 2008.

if the radiator has been removed in the past. The heater platform can rub on the inner bonnet surfaces. Cars built in the mid-2000s may have the bonnet inner faces painted in base coat only, or with a grey finish from new. Morgan reverted to finishing these as per the exterior from 2006. Check that air filter trunking has not excessively worn the inside of the bonnet, especially on the Rover-engined cars. The gap between the bonnet and the top of the wing should be consistent from side-to-side, though the gap is larger on later cars. Bonnet tape on all cars from 1986 should not be painted, but rather will be a natural material with a light coating of grease. Check the paintwork around the bonnet louvres, particularly on 1990s models, as the paint can flake off in this area due to poor etch priming.

Chassis, bulkhead and valances

Although covered in chapter 7, re-check these areas in more detail, looking for cracks, corrosion, and possible accident damage along the chassis rails. Examine the valances and bulkhead carefully, especially on pre-stainless steel cars. If a car is pre-1998 and has stainless valances it may well be that they have already been changed due to corrosion or accident damage. Fittings should be consistent on both sides of the car. Lots of fresh bolts or underseal on one side can indicate repairs ... investigate in more detail.

T16 chassis showing the five-speed gearbox.

Duratec chassis showing the battery position.

Brightwork condition

Anodised aluminium bumpers were standard fit until 1992. From 1992-1997, chrome bumpers were fitted as standard. Cars produced 1997-1998 had polished stainless steel bumpers, and, from 1998 on, stainless steel bumpers with end caps have been fitted. From 2003 there has been an option for overriders, and these are polished stainless steel. Check bumpers for damage, alignment and condition. Chrome bumpers from 1992 can corrode and pit quite badly, and discolour around the exhaust area. If overriders are fitted, check for impact damage.

High level brake light introduced in 1998 as part of 114 changes to meet type approval.

Anodised aluminium bumper.

Examine the inner and outer headlamp rims on all cars, as well as numberplate lamp covers and the door mirror bases and stems. These can all pit and corrode badly. The cost to replace is not excessive, but a good coat of wax polish will help protect them. Heavy use of chrome cleaners

Chrome bumper.

will remove the chrome over time (front grilles pre-2002 are particularly susceptible to showing the base coating). Post-2002 grilles are stainless. Make sure the grille slats are attached. Black grilles and meshes have been a factory option from 2012. Morgan refers to the grille as a stone guard on its pricelists.

There were several types of door mirrors fitted over time; the adjustable ones with the nut to adjust the height have been obsolete for years. The mirror heads are usually stainless but the bases and stems are not. Aftermarket items are available, including fully stainless with different mirror heads. Passenger mirrors were fitted as standard from 1998. Side lights on the wings were standard fit up until 2008, but have been optional since, as the sidelight is now mounted in the headlamp unit. Check any remaining chromework: aerials, where fitted, and luggage racks, for example. Most racks are now stainless steel.

Wood frame condition

Double-check your initial findings with regard to hinge post movement, loose tacks in the door threshold strips, and movement in the body joints. Saggy trim on the sillboards needs further investigation as this can indicate the padding has rotted causing the wood to deteriorate from the top rather than from underneath. Post-1986 wood frames are treated and give little trouble, but you should still check.

Windscreen condition

Studded windscreens were fitted up until 2003; later items are stud free. There's an option for a studded screen on the later models, though. Heated windscreens have been fitted as standard from 1998. It's difficult to check the operation, though, so you may need to ask the vendor. Windscreen glasses de-laminate with age – identified by a 'milky' edge around the outside of the glass, usually beginning around the lower corners. Check for wiper blade damage and stone chips, particularly around the interior mirror area, as they are easy to miss in this location.

Check that the glass fits the frame. Gaps at the bottom on repaired screens are not uncommon, and are usually hidden with sealant. Glasses are available or can be cut for the non heated screens. The usual practice for the heated windscreens is to change the whole windscreen. Morgan changed manufacturers, and the shape of the glass can vary to the frame. This is only evident when stripping down the assembly. These are very expensive, so make sure you have adequate windscreen cover on your insurance. Cracks in the glass can be caused by over-tight hoods or when owners pull on the frames to get in and out of the car. These usually start from the mounting screws (three per side).

Check the chromework around the screen and the mounting pillars for corrosion. Wind deflectors may have been fitted to the side of the windscreen; if the screws are too long cracks can occur. When sidescreens are fitted it is

Windscreens can crack, incur stone chips, and de-laminate. This screen has suffered all three.

easy to trap the deflectors when closing the door, thus cracked or broken deflectors are common. Glass deflectors are available and are mounted slightly differently.

Weather equipment

Although you would have already checked that the weather equipment fits, as mentioned in chapter 7, re-check the condition of each piece of weather equipment now. Look for fittings coming adrift, particularly the 'lift a dot' fasteners and 'turn button' plates on pre-2004 hoods and tonneaus. The hood stitching can pull apart at the front on the studded windscreen design, and it's not easy to repair without using a patch. The side of the hood towards the rear of the sidescreen area can split on both styles due to stretching when owners get in and out.

For later cars, check that the side Tenax fastener on the elbow panel is intact, and that it fits when the hood is up. It's common for hoods to be stored during the winter – this is recommended – but owners often forget to fit the Tenax so the hood can shrink in this area.

Tonneau cover.

Four-seater hood in mohair.

The header rail seal should be in place and not creased. Header rail side mount brackets can shear off at their weld point – usually due to over-tightening of the cant rail to stop rattles. Check that the rear frame locks in position and that the frame is not broken. Later four-seater models have a wooden upper front rail as part of the hood mechanism. Check that this front rail and the rear bar are in good condition, as they can rot. Check the sidescreen condition and that the lower pouch screws are there; they can fall out. Check that the sidescreen rubbers are in good condition.

Inside a four-seater with the hood up.

Interior condition

Re-check in more detail any areas of concern noted in your inspection from chapter 7. Check whether the interior has been re-dyed. If it has, the colour of the leather may look painted on rather than the natural finish. The odd area that has been treated for scuffs and wear is fine and can be expected on older examples. Lighter interiors may look more worn than darker interiors, though they can look roomier with the hood up. Stone and biscuit leather, although quite light, are quite practical colours as they don't show up dust and dirt as readily as darker colours. Don't assume you will be able to match any wear areas easily. Water stains or drips on the gearbox cover are common. This is usually due to the wiper spindle bezel gaskets not sealing – gently tightening the bezel nut can cure this issue.

Seat condition and operation

Two-seaters originally had fixed seatbacks with single-pin headrest holes (headrests were optional until 1998). A folding reclining seat was introduced on two-seaters as a cost option until 2000. These had a flat seatback and are referred to as tombstone seats. Sports seats were introduced as an option in 1995, these had a fixed-back with added side support and full seat tilt mechanism to enable you to access the rear storage area. The reclining sports seats have more side support, and became the standard seat in 2012. Seats are normally mounted on wooden blocks depending on when the car was built; if fitted, and if you need to raise the seat, you can add in taller blocks!

Four-seaters have always been fitted with folding reclining seats, with sports seats becoming standard from 2006.

Performance seats were introduced in 2012 for both models. These have

Optional folding reclining sports seat, standard fit from 2008.

Standard fixed-back seat.

Performance seat.

larger, deeper headrests, additional support areas, and inflatable lumbar support. Check that all mechanisms work.

Seat base webbings can collapse along the rubber membrane (you can lift the seat cushion on some seats to check this membrane). Seats with side supports tend to wear on the raised areas. Piping can wear, so check the backs of the seats.

For four-seaters, examine the rear seats; for the later 2006-on model ensure the rear seatbacks lock into position.

Seatbelt condition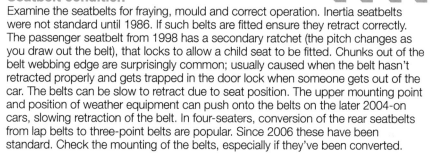
Examine the seatbelts for fraying, mould and correct operation. Inertia seatbelts were not standard until 1986. If such belts are fitted ensure they retract correctly. The passenger seatbelt from 1998 has a secondary ratchet (the pitch changes as you draw out the belt), that locks to allow a child seat to be fitted. Chunks out of the belt webbing edge are surprisingly common; usually caused when the belt hasn't retracted properly and gets trapped in the door lock when someone gets out of the car. The belts can be slow to retract due to seat position. The upper mounting point and position of weather equipment can push onto the belts on the later 2004-on cars, slowing retraction of the belt. In four-seaters, conversion of the rear seatbelts from lap belts to three-point belts are popular. Since 2006 these have been standard. Check the mounting of the belts, especially if they've been converted.

Carpets
Check the carpets. Are they wet, stained, moth damaged, threadbare or faded? Is there evidence of rodent damage? Rubber matting was fitted on the inside of the bulkhead until 1989, whereupon carpet has been fitted. Slide the seat forward and check underneath. Rear spring hanger leather may be damaged where the seat has been slid back. There is always a heel mat on the driver's side front footwell carpet. The front crossmember in front of the seat may be carpeted, have a stainless cover, or be exposed. Two carpet pieces have been supplied with new cars from 1998 to cover the crossmember on each side (these aren't factory fitted so the chassis number can be clearly seen for export purposes). Plus 4s up to the mid-1990s may have carpeted propshaft tunnel and sillboard covers. These would have been factory fitted at the owner's request, and are rarely found.

Dashboard and steering wheel
Leather or vinyl covered dashboards were standard up until 2008, whereupon painted dashboards became standard. Walnut dashboards have always been a popular option, and additional wood finishes were introduced from 2016. Up until 2007 walnut dashboards were supplied with lockable lids. Check that the lock works. A finger tab under the lock was removed in 1998 to meet European regulations, so you have to hold the key to open the lid on these later models Check the condition of the dashboard for bleaching and cracks, and examine the crash padding material for ring and fingernail damage.

A black, 15in steering wheel is standard, and the no-cost option of a 14in rim is a popular choice. Post-1998 steering wheels have a padded centre with the horn push in the middle. A lot of owners change to a Moto-Lita steering wheel, ideally fitted to the Moto-Lita boss. There is very little effect on the steering between a 15in or 14in wheel. If a 13in wheel is fitted, though, this will make the steering a little heavier. Check the steering wheel for excessive movement and play. Some owners pull on the

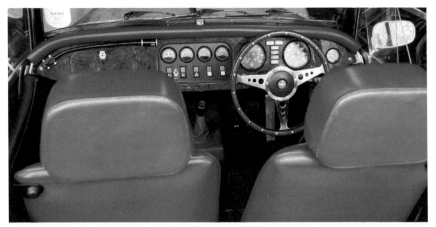

Dashboard to 1997.

steering wheel as they get in and out, and this can prematurely wear the top column bushes.

Airbags were an expensive cost option from 1998 and are quite rare. These airbag steering wheels are 16in in diameter. The passenger airbag is mounted in the glovebox behind a cover. Duratec cars were not offered with the option of airbags.

Steering columns have been adjustable from 1998, but are generally kept in the uppermost position. Some cars may have had an aftermarket modification to allow the column to tilt a little higher.

Dashboard electrics and gauges

Short-door cars have the dashboard at a slight angle, with the speedometer and rev counter in easy view. The oil pressure gauge, voltmeter, temperature gauge and fuel gauges are fitted in a row in the middle of the dashboard, with a series of switches mounted below. The individual gauges can mist up. In the early 1990s holes were drilled into the rear of the gauges to help prevent this. Rover-engined cars have the fuel tank unit in a tube. This can make the gauge a little unreliable due to an air gap in the top of the tank. The gauge can read just over three-quarters of a tank when full but will read empty accurately.

Fiat-engined cars have Lucas rocker switches which can now be quite fragile due to age. In 1986 the switches changed to VDO and are very reliable.

Long-door cars have the dashboard further back, and mounted vertically. This was to allow for the option of air bags. The demister pipes were removed to enable this, and a heated windscreen was fitted. The centre cluster has four gauges, the switches are not mounted beneath but in two groups, one on either side of the speedometer and rev counter. With a 14in steering wheel the speedometer can be a little difficult to read.

Duratec cars have had cream dials as standard from 2004. In November 2007 the dashboard layout changed with the heater controls being raised on to the dashboard. At this point the gauges reverted back to being black-faced. The dashboard layout changed again in 2014 when the GDI was launched. Special editions can have different dashboard finishes and layouts.

Late 1997 to 2000 dashboard.

Super Sport dashboard. Note rally clocks on gearbox tunnel and Brooklands steering wheel.

Standard factory steering wheel. Most owners change to a Moto-Lita steering wheel.

Duratec cream instruments fitted until November 2007. Check that the switch panel works correctly.

Plus 4 Super Sport dashboard has unique instruments and toggle switches.

Start the car and check that all gauges and dashboard warning lights work. The engine warning light (yellow engine symbol) on 1998-on cars should go out once the car is started. Digital display speedometers were fitted from 1996-2000. These can suffer due to damp/age, and the displays can stop working intermittently. Common issues are flickering, scrolling of the numbers, or the display going out alltogether. Dry, warm weather conditions can restore the unit in some instances. At the time of writing these units cannot be repaired, and new replacement units are unavailable, but similar speedo head units can be purchased. Any speedometer change should be noted in the vehicle history, along with the mileage at the point of change. The sealing rubbers can split and the gauges can work loose on their mounting plates.

In 2004-2007 cars, with cream dials, ensure that the indicators and hazard lamps work. Water ingress into the indicator lamps can cause a short circuit that damages the instrument panel circuit board. The switches are push button, and the fan switch on cars from 2004-2006 may have only one speed rather than two. Chrome gauge rims can split or tarnish.

The later gauges on 2014 GDI cars have had very few problems to date.

Check wiper and indicator stalks for security and operation. Check that the washers work, as the jet tubes can become detached and jets themselves can become clogged.

Interior controls, including pedals

Ensure that all controls work. Clutch and brake pedals should have rubbers fitted, or have an anti-slip finish. Clutch pedal springs can break and clevis pins can wear, so check for excessive 'slop' in the pedals. Check that the radio works, if fitted, remembering to pull up the aerial; electric aerials are rare.

Heater controls

Check that the heater controls work and that any flaps on the heater box move. Early cars have a pull cable to operate the heater valve. This is rarely used, so make sure it hasn't seized. Later cars have a turn knob on the heater box. The newer the car the better the heater operation. Heated seats have become a popular option in recent years, though they can take a little time to warm up. Check these with the engine running.

Keys and immobilisers

Each lock has its own key, so the fuel cap key will be different to the door key, for example, which will be different to the glovebox key. Fuel cap keys are LF keys, easy to remember as 'lead free,' door and glovebox keys are FS keys. The standard Rover ignition lock was fitted from 1985 to 2000. From 2004-on, a chipped ignition key has been used which turns off the immobiliser. There is a small plug in the black section of the key; ensure this is present on any spare

Late T16 immobiliser key fob and keys.

set. The ignition key changed in 2014, and, instead of a transponder ring around the key barrel, there is a wire attached to the column cowl. The wire can dislodge, causing the immobiliser not to disarm when the key is put in the barrel.

Each new car was supplied with two ignition keys, two fuel cap keys, two door keys and two glovebox keys (pre-2014). If the passenger side has a lock, an additional two keys would have been supplied. Ensure the door and glovebox keys fit and work.

T16 Rover cars from 1996 came with a key fob immobiliser. From 1998, the immobiliser self arms after a couple of minutes. There is a red dash lamp in the middle instrument cluster that flashes to confirm the system is active. A button is pressed on the fob to disarm the system before putting the key in the ignition. It takes a few moments for the system to deactivate, so racing starts should be avoided. If the system has not deactivated properly, it will crank the starter motor but the engine will not fire. Once disarmed, though, turn on the ignition, allow the fuel pump to buzz and build up pressure, then start the car. There is an additional glitch with this system: you may also find, on cranking the car, that the starter motor sounds very slow, as though the battery is flat. The system can cause the ignition timing to over-advance, so turn off the ignition and try again; normal cranking speed should resume.

Wiper operation and blade condition   4   3   2   1

Check that the wipers and washers work on all speeds, and that pre-1998 stalks are not loose in the switch housing. Post-1998 switches are very reliable. Washer pumps and jets can block up with sediment from washer fluid due to lack of use. The wipers are best described as adequate. From 1977, three wiper blades were fitted to the car for improved visibility. Check the blade rubbers for splitting. When checking the operation, make sure that the wipers park in the lower position when turned off; the motor park switches can fail.

Wheels and tyres   4   3   2   1

Grey-painted 15in wire wheels are fitted as standard, and tyres should be 195/60x15. Chrome wire wheels, stainless wheels, deeper black wires and Roadster 16in stainless wires can be fitted. If chrome or stainless wires have been fitted and the car has a spare wheel cover, check that the spare matches. Examine wheel condition; loose spokes are not usually an issue. Avon tyres were the original fit until 2000, Yokohamas are the current standard fit. Check tyres carefully for age-related cracks. Morgans are good on tyre wear, though hardening and flat-spotting due to lack of use are common.

Rear suspension and brakes   4   3   2   1

Leaf springs are fitted to the rear. Two-seaters were fitted with five-leaf springs as standard, but, as these can sag quite quickly, six-leaf items have been a popular replacement option. In 2009 four-leaf springs were introduced. Earlier four-seaters have seven-leaf springs, but you may find they have been converted to six-leaf.

Lever arm shock absorbers were standard fit until 1992, whereupon they changed over to a telescopic shock absorber arrangement mounted on a brace bar that helps to stiffen the chassis. If you're able to lift out the rear luggage board on pre-Duratec cars you can see the axle and rear suspension. This is ideal for a quick check of the shock absorbers.

Optional Plus 8 alloy wheel.

Optional 16in Roadster stainless wire wheel.

Super Sport Minilite alloy wheel.

Have a look at the handbrake linkage and the rear brake backplates. The paper gaskets can weep, but wetness here could also be a sign of hub seal failure. Later BTR axles (post-1996) are less prone to hub seal leaks. Rear brakes went from manual adjustment (Girling) to self-adjusting (AP) brakes in 1993. The handbrake moved from the left side to the right at this time, but moved back to the left on Plus 4s from 2004.

The handbrake is of the fly-off type. You should be able to pull the handbrake up three clicks for it to lock in place on earlier cars. On later cars there's more movement so four to five clicks to the locking position is normal. You should not hear the clicks during normal operation of the handbrake, as this prematurely wears out the ratchet. The correct method for applying the handbrake is as follows: pull the lever back towards you until you have a fair bit of tension, push down the button on the top, and move the lever forward, you will feel the handbrake lock in place; it's now on. To release, pull the lower part of the lever towards you, the spring-loaded button will pop up, and the lever will then travel easily toward the front of the car; hence the term 'fly-off.' The levers can rub on the handbrake gaiter, so you may need to assist it to the fully off position. Turn on the ignition and check that the warning light goes out.

Rear wheel cylinders are prone to leaking and seizure on later Duratec cars. If they are seized, and the vehicle is on level ground, try to push the car backwards and forwards. You may feel the rear brakes grab, or the car could be very hard to push. It's common for the rear brakes to pass a UK MOT even with sticking cylinders. Subsequent removal of the drums will enable you to assess the problem. Check the service

Gearbox tunnel on a T16 model showing handbrake and early
radio-mounting position.

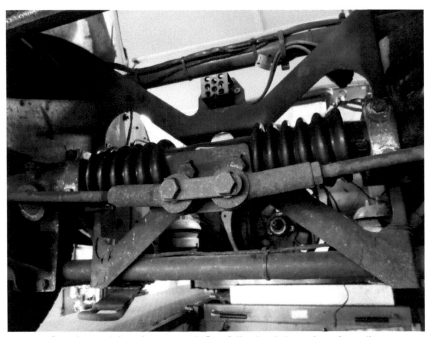

Steering rack is quite exposed. Carefully check the gaiters for splits.

Lever arm rear shock absorber.

history. If there's no record of cylinder changes you may need to budget for this. At the dealership we have to put cylinders on over 70 per cent of the later cars we sell during handover preparation.

Exhaust

From 1998 the factory fitted stainless steel exhausts from the downpipe back, and catalytic converters have been fitted since 1992. These, too, are stainless, but have steel flanges and clamps which can corrode badly as they are behind the front wheel and, thus, are exposed to the elements. Centre boxes can crack where the pipework enters and exits the silencer, baffles can work loose, and exhaust mountings split with age. Rover-engined Plus 4s used to have a mild steel rear silencer box that curved up inside the rear wing, very few of these will have survived; replacements have a straight through pipe. There are various aftermarket performance exhaust systems available. Be careful of cars that have had the catalytic converters removed, or been replaced by a sports cat. These can be harder to get through emissions testing.

Front suspension

The Morgan sliding pillar arrangement is legendary. Dating back to 1909, all the Plus 4s in this book use it.

The stub axle is fitted with an upper and lower bush, and slides on the kingpin. A main spring is fitted above the stub axle, and a rebound spring below. Check that the springs are not broken, and that the stub axle rests on the rebound spring.

Exhaust catalyst. Mounting flanges can crack and corrode away.

Stub axle assembly clearly showing the main spring, shock absorber and rod end with grease nipple.

Kingpin assembly, showing steering rack track rod and end. Rebound spring and damper blade makes this car pre-2005.

Cars up to 2005 have a bronze thrust plate between the main spring and stub axle base. If this is not lubricated properly the steering can become very tight. The thin damper blade behind absorbs some of the shock going through the system. This can need adjusting on service, and can click when the steering is turned. Cars up to 2000 were fitted with an oiler valve which releases engine oil via a thin pipe to the top of the kingpins. Every 500-750 miles the valve should be pressed when the engine is started but still cold. Some owners do not use the oiler system. Additional grease nipples are fitted to grease the suspension more regularly. The oiler valve was phased out in 2000.

From 2005 roller bearings replaced the thrust plates fitted on the earlier cars. These improve the self centring of the steering. If you're able to safely raise up the front of the car (ideally on axle stands) you can check for wheel bearing play, kingpin wear, and play in the trackrod ends.

With the front wheel directly in front of you, hold it at the 1 o'clock and 7 o'clock positions to check for movement. You may feel a small amount of play – this may just be in the wheel bearing. Next, hold the wheel at the 11 o'clock and 5 o'clock positions and check for movement. Finally, hold the wheel at the 6 o'clock position, and pull it back and forth. Watch the tyre as you move it, you should have no more than ½in (13mm) movement at the bottom. If there is play any movement will be noticeable, and you may even hear a 'clonk.' Get the vendor to assist so you can check behind the wheel at the stub axle for movement, if any was detected during the checks.

Check the trackrod ends for play by holding the front of the wheel at the 9 o'clock and 3 o'clock positions. I've found that, with the car on the ground, gripping and rocking the top of the wheel to check for kingpin wear is pointless, unless the bushes are very badly worn (you would no doubt have noticed uneven tyre wear if this was the case – evident as wear on the outside of the tread similar to having too much positive camber). A little movement in the kingpins does not mean they need changing immediately, they could last several thousand more miles.

Various types of kingpins are available, including stainless steel and hardened chrome. There are many opinions on which types to fit, and whether you should grease or use the oiler valve. At this stage all you're looking for is excessive play and whether the car will need a front end overhaul in the next few years. Some cars may have the increasingly popular option of the Suplex/SSL front suspension. This has adjustable platforms and springs to allow more progressive spring and suspension travel, and can improve the ride, particularly over potholes. Adjustable shock absorbers are also a popular upgrade.

Front brakes   4 3 2 1

Given the age range of cars covered by this book, the front brakes will likely be non-vented disc brakes. Although harder to check on alloy-wheeled cars, look at the brake discs for scoring, 'bluing' of the contact surface (this indicates excessive heat from sticking caliper pistons), and for wear lips. Look from behind the wheel to check the inner faces of the discs, they can become quite pitted with rust. Discs are a Morgan only part, but can be skimmed if there is only light wear.

Later cars with very low mileage can develop brake disc judder. Check for this on the road test.

Since 2004 Plus 4s have been fitted with four-pot brake calipers. Uprated brake kits are sometimes fitted, and these may include drilled/cross-drilled discs. Servo assistance wasn't standard until late 1992, so the brake pedal may feel harder than on a modern vehicle, and more pedal effort may be needed to stop. Visually check the brake hoses on lock-to-lock for condition and fouling.

Steering   4 3 2 1

A Gemmer steering box was fitted until December 1991. Check it for leaks and a smooth operation. Rack and pinion was initially a no cost option, before becoming standard in 1991. Check operation for smoothness, and ask the seller to wiggle the steering wheel from side-to-side so you can check steering joints between the column and the rack, and for excessive play in the rack. Rack gaiters split, and these are quite expensive, as can the rack end caps.

During the wiggle test check for play and movement in the track rod joints. The inner steering rack joints can wear. Trackrod gaiters can split with age and are now a UK MOT failure point.

Toolkit   4 3 2 1

If the car is fitted with a spare wheel, the toolkit will consist of a jack with handle, hammer, and a spanner for wire-wheeled cars. If the car has alloy wheels the toolkit includes a jack with handle and a wheel wrench. Sport models do not have a spare wheel, so the tool bag will have a can of tyre sealant, a hammer, and a spanner. Since 2004 the toolkit has been situated in a felt-lined tray under a thin board behind the seats on the luggage shelf area. Check the tray for impact damage from the axle. Earlier cars will have the toolkit mounted in the toolbox on the bulkhead. Later four-seaters have the toolkit in a bag in the storage area behind the folding rear seats.

Exterior lights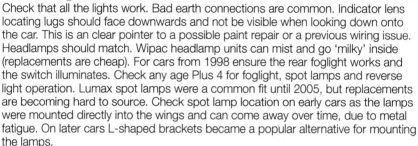
Check that all the lights work. Bad earth connections are common. Indicator lens locating lugs should face downwards and not be visible when looking down onto the car. This is an clear pointer to a possible paint repair or a previous wiring issue. Headlamps should match. Wipac headlamp units can mist and go 'milky' inside (replacements are cheap). For cars from 1998 ensure the rear foglight works and the switch illuminates. Check any age Plus 4 for foglight, spot lamps and reverse light operation. Lumax spot lamps were a common fit until 2005, but replacements are becoming hard to source. Check spot lamp location on early cars as the lamps were mounted directly into the wings and can come away over time, due to metal fatigue. On later cars L-shaped brackets became a popular alternative for mounting the lamps.

Right-hand engine bay
With the bonnet open check the condition of the top of the bulkhead, toolbox, if fitted, fusebox area, inner valance, chassis crossmember, wiring and hoses. Check overall engine bay condition. Is it clean and tidy or does it look neglected? Light oxidisation of aluminium castings is to be expected. Re-check for evidence of overspray.

Early T16 engine bay, powder-coated bulkhead and black engine block. M16s have a red block.

Duratec engine bay. Note the air filter and rocker cover compared to the GDI.

Left-hand engine bay

As per the right-hand side, check the engine components, bulkhead, valance and exhaust for condition, and score accordingly.

Cooling system

Check the coolant level when the engine is cold. Plus 4s in the age range covered by this book will have an expansion tank so the coolant level may be clearly visible. Blue antifreeze is normal on cars up to 2000, and red antifreeze from 2004. The Rover-engined models have a metal expansion tank. Remove the cap to look inside, check there is coolant in the tank, but ignore the level tag as they find a natural level. Dip the coolant to check the colour and ask when the antifreeze was last changed.

Blue antifreeze can go 'milky' with age, and can clog up the radiator tubes. Red antifreeze can go a rust colour, and can completely stain the expansion bottle. In either circumstance a flush and antifreeze change is required. Check for leaks as part of your engine bay checks; radiators are prone to leaking.

Duratec GDI engine bay.

Battery

On two-seaters the battery is mounted behind the left-hand front seat, accessible by an access panel under the rear board. If a sealed gel-type battery is fitted, these are located on the bulkhead in the engine bay. On four-seaters the battery may be fitted on either side, depending on age, under the rear seat. Access for changing and checking the battery can be tricky. Type 038/015 batteries were fitted as standard up until 2000.

A gel-type sealed battery was fitted from 2004. These are expensive and can last as little as two years if not regularly used/charged. Morgan went back to a standard type battery in October 2005. Batteries run down over a period of time if the car is not used, so connecting to a battery conditioner is recommended. A cigar lighter socket/auxiliary socket is an ideal connection point due to the location of the battery and the fact that the sockets are permanently live.

Cigar lighters were optional on the earlier cars and usually mounted in the glovebox. Most early Duratec cars will have a cigar lighter fitted. From 2007, an auxiliary socket has been fitted under the dashboard as standard.

Battery conditioners are plugged in and left on the car to keep the battery fully charged. Their use can disguise the true state of a battery over five years old, though, and when disconnected the battery could go flat very quickly. Check the history/ask the vendor to provide proof if the car has had a recent battery change.

Clutch
Clutches are cable-operated on the Fiat models, and hydraulically operated on the rest of the cars covered by this guide. Check the fluid reservoir on Rover-engined Plus 4s as the cylinders can leak. Later models have very few problems.

The clutch should have a smooth pedal action with the bite point just over halfway. There should be no 'sponginess,' and the cars are not prone to clutch slip or judder. Clutches rarely wear out despite most owners resting their clutch foot lightly on the pedal. Some release bearing noise is to be expected which will reduce once the pedal is depressed, and some light gearbox bearing noise can normally be heard as there is very little soundproofing.

Under-bonnet brakes
Servo brakes were not fitted until late 1992. Check brake fluid level and condition of the master cylinder. Brake pipe routing should be neat and tidy.

Engine, gearbox and axle
Complete your visual checks of the engine, including checking the oil level. Start the car and listen for abnormal noises. Look underneath to check for fluid leaks at the back of the gearbox. On the Rover gearboxes the fifth speed housing gaskets weep. MX5 gearbox rear seals and front pinion seals on the axles can leak. It is worth checking for dampness and staining around the fuel tank and for strong fuel smells. Fuel tanks on older cars can leak at the seams, and the fuel filler hoses can perish badly on later cars.

Rover engines have a rubber throttle body mounting plate which can deteriorate and suck in air causing misfires and rough running.

Test drive
If all's well so far it's now test drive time. Evaluate the following:

Cold start
Make sure the car idles once started, and, as you pull away, check for misfires. Check that the car runs well from cold (particularly Rover-engined cars). As the ECU changes from the cold start to warm cycle, drive on light throttle and monitor whether the car lurches or tries to cut out. A circuit board fault in the ECU can cause issues at this particular time. Once hot it can run fine. GDI engines rev high and then settle on start-up; this is a normal purging characteristic. GDI engines from 2018 can feel a little flat between 2000-3000rpm, this is normal (increase throttle pressure to compensate).

Gearbox operation
Fiat gearboxes are very precise when changing gear. Rover gearboxes can be notchy, with the synchros being a bit slow on the first few changes. As soon as the oil circulates and warms up, though, the gear change should improve. Later R380 'boxes have a slightly smoother/easier change. Ford gearboxes, fitted up to 2010,

Sump and servo location on a T16 model. Note the triangular plate attached to the crossmember; these can corrode.

Duratec engine bay clearly showing the driver's side valance.

Rear axle on M16 and T16 models. Note axle drain plug and how dry the pinion seal at front is. They are usually wet.

Leaf springs are fitted at the rear, this car has telescopic rear shock absorbers.

can be notchy until they have covered a high mileage. MX5 gearboxes are smooth. Check for abnormal noises during driving or changing gear. Make sure you go up and down the 'box, including fifth and reverse.

Steering

You'll get a lot of feel and feedback through the steering. It will be heavier at lower speed or when manoeuvring as most will not have power steering. It should have the same feel from side-to-side. A rubbing sound on full lock is normally due to the tyre rubbing on the block mounted on the chassis and should be expected on cars up to 2000. Check for wheel shake at 50-60mph, which could be due to wheel balance. Progressive vibration through the steering or strange handling could be flat-spotted tyres.

Noises, clonks, rattles and squeaks
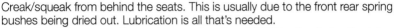
Look out for the following:

Creak/squeak from behind the seats. This is usually due to the front rear spring bushes being dried out. Lubrication is all that's needed.

A light 'clonk' as you pull away is normal on the old GKN axles, being the take-up in the prop and diff. This is quite normal. There shouldn't be a clonk on the later axles.

A click from the wheel area as you pull away can mean the wheels have not been tightened sufficiently on the hubs and the wheel is moving on the spline – this is common if the owner has removed the wheels to clean them.

Sidescreens rattle and can squeak against the elbow panel; those on four-seaters can potentially rattle more.

Luggage rack bars and exhausts can rattle. Bonnets and front spots (if fitted) can vibrate. Minor adjustment may be all that's required.

Creaking from the front. The upper wing stays can break and cause a creak whilst driving.

A whistling noise from the windscreen area could be the screen. Headlamp rims can also cause a loud whistle.

Lever arm shock absorbers are noisy in operation compared to telescopic shockers.

Noisy fan belts can be caused by antifreeze from a previous radiator leak dropping on the belt, so re-check this area after the road test.

Rotational clonking/scraping noise from rear when cornering can, in some instances, be the propshaft rubbing on the surrounding housing.

Rattling noise from Rover T16 engines in the area of the auxiliary belt can be caused by the dummy power steering pump that drives the water pump. Replacements are getting hard to source.

Performance and handling

You should be pleasantly surprised by the ride; it's not as hard as people sometimes claim. It's often mentioned that it feels as if you're travelling 10mph faster than you are actually going. The car should pull sweetly in all gears; the tuned limited edition versions feel very different on the road and will be very sprightly. However, you should be able to drive smoothly at all speeds, whether pottering around, or enthusiastically driving along country lanes.

Check for drifting to one side, particularly under braking conditions. Sticking calipers or even under-inflated tyres can cause this. Check for vibration through the brake pedal, which is likely due to warped brake discs. Non-servo brakes take a little getting used to. ABS is not fitted to any of the models. Within a short time you'll get used to the pedals coming up from the floor.

The car should feel predictable and stable even when driven in a spirited fashion. If not it will need further investigation. Please remember, a Plus 4 will feel like a cross between a 1960s classic and a modern car; this is part of the charm.

Instruments

Check that they all work, particularly the temperature and fuel gauges. If there's a digital display check it's displaying clearly. Gauges can mist up internally. The oil gauges can move through quite a range, but check the needle isn't going straight over to maximum (the sensor can short internally). We rarely have issues with poor oil pressure. Do the indicators self cancel? Engine temperature should be between 85-100 degrees. Are any warning lights illuminated?

Final hot checks

I hope you have enjoyed your road test. Now, with the engine idling, check the temperature gauge, and under the bonnets again for leaks and for smoke from the exhaust. Leave the engine running until the coolant fan kicks in; this is usually just over 100 degrees. Once it cuts out again turn off the engine. If you noticed any pulling or drifting on the steering carefully check each wheel for temperature by placing your hand on the centre hub. They should all be about the same. Leave it for a few minutes and then restart the car to ensure it will start when hot, and to recheck the engine bay in case you've missed anything. Turn off the engine one last time and then evaluate your scores.

Evaluation procedure

Add up the total points.

Score: 156 = excellent; 117 = good; 78 = average; 39 = poor.

Cars scoring over 109 will be completely usable and will require only maintenance and care to preserve condition. Cars scoring between 39 and 80 will require some serious work (at much the same cost regardless of score). Cars scoring between 81 and 108 will require very careful assessment of the necessary repair/restoration costs in order to arrive at a realistic value.

Check	Page	Rating			
Paint	40	4	3	2	1
Body tub panels and rear wings	40	4	3	2	1
Front wings, bonnets and cowl	42	4	3	2	1
Chassis, bulkhead and valances	44	4	3	2	1
Brightwork condition	45	4	3	2	1
Wood frame condition	46	4	3	2	1
Windscreen condition	46	4	3	2	1
Weather equipment	47	4	3	2	1
Interior condition	48	4	3	2	1
Seat condition and operation	48	4	3	2	1
Seatbelt condition	49	4	3	2	1
Carpets	49	4	3	2	1
Dashboard and steering wheel	49	4	3	2	1
Dashboard electrics and gauges	50	4	3	2	1
Interior controls, including pedals	53	4	3	2	1
Heater controls	53	4	3	2	1
Keys and immobilisers	53	4	3	2	1
Wiper operation and blade condition	54	4	3	2	1
Wheels and tyres	54	4	3	2	1
Rear suspension and brakes	54	4	3	2	1
Exhaust	57	4	3	2	1
Front suspension	57	4	3	2	1
Front brakes	60	4	3	2	1
Steering	60	4	3	2	1
Toolkit	60	4	3	2	1
Exterior lights	61	4	3	2	1
Right-hand engine bay	61	4	3	2	1
Left-hand engine bay	62	4	3	2	1
Cooling system	62	4	3	2	1
Battery	63	4	3	2	1
Clutch	64	4	3	2	1
Under-bonnet brakes	64	4	3	2	1
Engine, gearbox and axle	64	4	3	2	1
Test drive	64				
Cold start	64	4	3	2	1
Gearbox operation	64	4	3	2	1
Steering	65	4	3	2	1
Noises, clonks, rattles and squeaks	66	4	3	2	1
Performance and handling	66	4	3	2	1
Instruments	66	4	3	2	1
Final hot checks	67	4	3	2	1
Total					

10 Auctions

– sold! Another way to buy your dream

Plus 4 four-seater. A good example previously sold at auction.

Auction pros & cons
Pros: Prices will usually be lower than those of dealers or private sellers. Clear title will have been established, and you can usually examine documents relating to the vehicle.
Cons: You have to rely on a basic description of condition and history, the opportunity to inspect is limited, and you can't drive the car. Cars are often a little below par and may require some work. It's easy to overbid, and there's usually a buyer's premium.

Which auction?
Auctions by established auctioneers are advertised in car magazines and on the auctioneers' websites. A catalogue, or a simple list of the lots might only be available a day or two ahead, though may be listed and pictured earlier online. Ask the company if previous selling prices are available (details of past sales are often available online).

Catalogue, entry fee and payment details
When you purchase the auction catalogue, it often acts as a ticket allowing two people to attend the viewing days and the auction. Catalogue details tend to be comparatively brief, but will include information such as 'one owner from new, low mileage, full service history,' etc. It will also usually show a guide price, and will specify the 'Buyer's premium.' It will also contain details of acceptable forms of payment.

At the fall of the hammer an immediate deposit is usually required, the balance payable within 24 hours. Note that there may be a lmit to how much can be paid in cash. Some auctions will accept payment by debit card. Sometimes credit or charge cards are acceptable, but may incur an extra charge. A bank draft or bank transfer will have to be arranged in advance with your own bank as well as with the auction house. No car will be released before all payments are cleared. If delays occur in payment transfers then storage costs can accrue.

Buyer's premium

Note that a buyer's premium will be added to the hammer price. It's not usual for there to be a further state or local tax on the purchase price and/or the buyer's premium.

Viewing

It may be possible to view on the day or days before, as well as in the hours prior to the auction. Officials can help by opening engine and luggage compartments and to allow you to inspect the interior. While they may start the engine, a test drive is out of the question. Crawling under and around the car as much as you want is permitted, but you can't have the car jacked up. You can ask to see any documentation.

Bidding

Decide on your maximum bid beforehand, and stick to it! It may take a while for the auctioneer to reach 'your' lot, so use the time to note how other bidders behave. When it's the turn of your car, attract the auctioneer's attention and make an early bid. He or she will then look to you for a reaction every time another bid is made. Usually the bids will be in fixed increments until the bidding slows, when smaller increments will often be accepted before the hammer falls. If you want to withdraw from the bidding a vigorous shake of the head when the auctioneer looks to you next should do the trick!

Assuming that you're the successful bidder, the auctioneer will note your card or paddle number, and you will then be responsible for the vehicle. If the car is unsold, because it failed to reach the reserve or because there was little interest, it may be possible to negotiate with the owner, via the auctioneers, after the sale is over.

Successful bid

There are two more items to consider: how to get the car home; and insurance. If you can't drive the car, your own/a hired trailer is one way, another is to have the vehicle shipped. The auction house will have details of specialist transport companies.

Insurance can usually be purchased on-site, but it may be more cost-effective to arrange it with your insurance company in advance, and then call to confirm the details.

eBay & other online auctions?

eBay and other online auctions could land you a car at a bargain price, but don't bid without examining the car first; something most vendors encourage. A useful feature of eBay is that the geographical location of the car is shown, so you can narrow down your choices to within a realistic radius of home. Be prepared to be outbid in the last few moments of the auction. Remember, your bid is binding and that it will be very difficult to get restitution in the case of a crooked vendor fleecing you – caveat emptor!

Some cars offered for sale in online auctions are 'ghost' cars. Don't part with any cash without being sure that the vehicle does actually exist and is as described.

Auctioneers

Barrett-Jackson www.barrett-jackson.com/
Bonhams www.bonhams.com/
British Car Auctions BCA) www.bca-europe.com or www.british-car-auctions.co.uk/
Cheffins www.cheffins.co.uk/
Christies www.christies.com/
Coys www.coys.co.uk/
eBay www.eBay.com/
H&H www.classic-auctions.co.uk/
RM www.rmauctions.com/
Shannons www.shannons.com.au/
Silver www.silverauctions.com

11 Paperwork

– correct documentation is essential!

A typical service history.

The paper trail

Classic, collector and prestige cars usually come with a large portfolio of paperwork, accumulated and passed on by a succession of proud owners. This documentation represents the real history of the car, and from it can be deduced the level of care the car has received, how much it's been used, which specialists have worked on it and the dates of major repairs and restorations. All of this information will be priceless to you as the new owner, so be very wary of cars with little paperwork to support their claimed history.

Registration documents

All countries/states have some form of registration for private vehicles, whether it's like the American 'pink slip' system or the British 'log book' system.

It is essential to check that the registration document is genuine, that it relates to the car in question, and that all the vehicle's details are correctly recorded, including chassis/VIN and engine numbers (if these are shown). If you are buying from the previous owner, his or her name and address will be recorded in the document: this will not be the case if you are buying from a dealer.

In the UK the current (Euro-aligned) registration document is named 'V5C,' and is printed in coloured sections of blue, green and pink. The blue section relates to the car specification, the green section has details of the new owner, and the pink section is sent to the DVLA in the UK when the car is sold. A small section in yellow deals with selling the car within the motor trade.

Previous ownership records

Due to the introduction of important new legislation on data protection, it's no longer possible to acquire, from the British DVLA, a list of previous owners of a car you own, or are intending to purchase. This scenario will also apply to dealerships and other specialists, from whom you may wish to make contact and acquire information on previous ownership and work carried out.

If the car has a foreign registration, there may be expensive and time-consuming formalities to complete. Do you really want the hassle?

Roadworthiness certificate

Most country/state administrations require that vehicles are regularly tested to prove that they are safe to use on the public highway and do not produce excessive emissions. In the UK that test (the 'MOT') is carried out at approved testing stations, for a fee. In the USA the requirement varies, but most states insist on an emissions test every two years as a minimum, while the police are charged with pulling over unsafe-looking vehicles.

In the UK the test is required on an annual basis once a vehicle becomes three years old. Of particular relevance for older cars is that the certificate issued includes the mileage reading recorded at the test date and, therefore, becomes an independent record of that car's history. Ask the seller if previous certificates are available. Without an MOT the vehicle should be trailered to its new home, unless you insist that a valid MOT is part of the deal. (Not such a bad idea this, as at least you will know the car was roadworthy on the day it was tested and you don't need to wait for the old certificate to expire before having the test done.)

In the UK, vehicles over 40 years old on May 20th each year, are exempt from MOT testing. Owners can still have the test carried out if they so wish.

Road licence

The administration of every country/state charges some kind of tax for the use of its road system, the actual form of the road licence, and how it is displayed, varying enormously country-to-country and state-to-state.

Whatever the form of the 'road licence,' it must relate to the vehicle carrying it and must be present and valid if the car is to be driven on the public highway legally.

Changed legislation in the UK means that the seller of a car must surrender any existing road fund licence, and it is the responsibility of the new owner to re-tax the vehicle at the time of purchase and before the car can be driven on the road. It's therefore vital to see the Vehicle Registration Certificate (V5C) at the time of purchase, and to have access to the New Keeper Supplement (V5C/2), allowing the buyer to obtain road tax immediately.

In the UK, classic vehicles 40 years old or more, on the 1st January each year get free road tax. It is still necessary to renew the tax status every year, even if there is no change.

If the car is untaxed because it has not been used for a period of time, the owner has to inform the licensing authorities.

Certificates of authenticity

For many makes of collectible car it's possible to get a certificate proving the age and authenticity (eg engine and chassis numbers, paint colour and trim) of a particular vehicle, these are sometimes called 'Heritage Certificates,' and, if the car comes with one of these, it's a definite bonus. If you want to obtain one, the relevant owners' club is the best starting point.

If the car has been used in European classic car rallies it may have a FIVA (Fédération Internationale des Véhicules Anciens) certificate. The so-called 'FIVA Passport,' or 'FIVA Vehicle Identity Card,' enables organisers and participants to recognise whether or not a particular vehicle is suitable for individual events. If you want to obtain such a certificate go to <www.fbhvc.co.uk> or <www.fiva.org>. There will be similar organisations in other countries.

Valuation certificate

Hopefully, the vendor will have a recent valuation certificate, or letter signed by a recognised expert stating how much he, or she, believes the particular car to be worth (such documents, together with photos, are usually needed to get 'agreed value' insurance). Generally such documents should act only as confirmation of your own assessment of the car, rather than a guarantee of value, as the expert has probably not seen the car in the flesh. The easiest way to find out how to obtain a formal valuation is to contact the owners' club.

Service history

Often these cars will have been serviced at home by enthusiastic (and hopefully capable) owners for a good number of years. Nevertheless, try to obtain as much service history and other paperwork pertaining to the car as you can. Naturally, dealer stamps, or specialist garage receipts score most points in the value stakes. However, anything helps in the great authenticity game. Items like the original bill of sale, handbook, parts invoices and repair bills, adding to the story and the character of the car. Even a brochure correct to the year of the car's manufacture is a useful document, and is something that you could well have to search hard to locate in future years. If the seller claims that the car has been restored, then expect receipts and other evidence from a specialist restorer.

If the seller claims to have carried out regular servicing, ask what work was completed, when, and seek some evidence of it being carried out. Your assessment of the car's overall condition should tell you whether the seller's claims are genuine.

Restoration photographs

If the seller tells you that the car has been restored, then expect to be shown a series of photographs taken while the restoration was under way. Pictures taken at various stages, and from various angles, should help you gauge the thoroughness of the work. If you buy the car, ask if you can have all the photographs, as they form an important part of the vehicle's history. However, it's surprising how many sellers are happy to part with their car and accept your cash, but want to hang on to their photographs! In the latter event, you may be able to persuade the vendor to get a set of copies made.

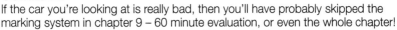

12 What's it worth?
– let your head rule your heart

Condition
If the car you're looking at is really bad, then you'll have probably skipped the marking system in chapter 9 – 60 minute evaluation, or even the whole chapter!

If you used the marking system, you'll know whether the car is in Excellent (maybe concours), Good, Average, or Poor condition, or somewhere in-between these categories. You're now faced with the task of deciding what you are prepared to pay.

A wealth of information can be found in various magazines and websites. The Morgan website car search is an excellent starting point, and gives the prices being asked for equivalent-aged models. Look at your budget and see what's available within it. The Plus 4 keeps its value extremely well, so expected values tend to be known by vendors and purchasers alike.

The value of the car is determined by the package as a whole: colour, condition, extras and history. Magazine price guides are not really reliable due to the age ranges they cover, and the fact that they don't take into account the range and cost of extras that can be fitted (potentially up to £12,000 on some examples). Morgans do not feature in the motor trade Cap 'black book' or Glasses guides.

Private sellers will ask about the same price as dealers, and, in some cases, more, as they believe their car is superior or they think they know the marketplace. You are not actually paying a premium at a dealership; you're paying for the security of knowing the car has been inspected, serviced, and supplied with a warranty. In addition, they can deal with your possible part-exchange and assist with finance if required. A private vendor will rarely offer any of the above. Auction houses may offer some of the features a dealer can offer, but you'll need to check their terms. Based on this, you should have more scope to negotiate with a private sale. Check photographs of the car, not just to look at the car itself but for clues to how long it's been on the market (foliage in the background, for example, can give a good indication).

Tastes change over time. For example, green and red were the most popular colours up until the early 1990s, so it'll be harder to find a blue example in this age range. Black wire wheels are a recent option, and can give the car quite a different look.

Desirable options/extras
Every Morgan is different, and a lot depends on the look an owner wanted to achieve. Some prefer a plain look, whilst others must have every option. The usual extras are chrome/stainless wire wheels, walnut dashboard, Moto-Lita steering wheel, and luggage racks. There is also a massive range of other options and aftermarket accessories available.

Undesirable features
Homemade accessories or genuine accessories poorly fitted can spoil the car, in terms of both looks and value. Buyers will often be deterred by a roll bar, assuming that it has been used on track or in competition, which may not be the case.

Repaired insurance write-offs need to be carefully examined, and will never be worth top money.

New car dealer specification box. All the samples from which to choose your ideal Plus 4.

Wind deflectors and a folding windscreen kit. Just some of the accessories that owners fit.

Luggage racks are a popular option.

A brand new car fitted with a Vitesse automatic conversion.

Super Sport bonnet scoop.

Front valances and spot lamps give the car a very different appearance.

Striking a deal

There are always some Plus 4s available, with limited editions being rare. Cars are now advertised to a worldwide audience, so you may need to be quick. Do not go to look at a car unless you are prepared to pay the asking price. Do not ask what the best price is before you have even viewed the car – this can give the impression that you are not a serious buyer. Private sales tend to have a little more flexibility, dealers possibly less so. While negotiating the deal, consider what you might want to add to the car over the coming years. Additional optional extras fitted prior to collection could be a good area to haggle on. For example, the dealer may be prepared to fit accessories within the asking price, or be prepared to split the costs for them. This can be a win win situation, helping the dealer secure a sale and you to save costs in the future.

13 Do you really want to restore?
– it'll take longer and cost more than you think

Do not underestimate the amount of work and time required to repair a vehicle as badly damaged as this.

Are you the 'hands-on' type, and do you have plenty of free time? If so, that restoration project you have seen may be just the ticket. Rolling restorations allow you to concentrate on certain areas over a number of months/years – for example engine bay detailing one year, part re-trim the next – allowing you to use the car in the interim. You'll pay more for one of these cars, but at least it will be complete and basically roadworthy, although still in need of work.

A basket case or dismantled car restoration will be a major undertaking, requiring a lot of time, money and space. Labour will be the biggest factor, and is likely to take twice the number of hours you think. Budget for between 200-400 hours to do a restoration well. A professional restorer or established Morgan dealer will be able to tackle the whole project for you. Be clear on what you want to achieve, though, and research and decide upon any upgrades before you get heavily involved in the work.

You may wish to go the DIY route, which has pros and cons. Either way you'll be putting a car that deserves saving back on the road, but ensure what is done is done well. Attention to detail is key – wings cut in nicely, the correct type of fixings, number of fixings per panel, etc – otherwise a future buyer may have to strip it down and start again.

This chassis should not be straightened. The impact force will travel down the complete chassis causing ripples along its length.

Pros: You can choose the colour and trim just like when ordering a new Morgan. Morgans can change colours several times over their lifetimes, and it's not detrimental to the value. You'll gain new skills, meet great people whilst sourcing parts, and get huge satisfaction as the project comes together. As most parts are readily available, and given the nature of construction of a Plus 4, the project can come together quickly, and require only a limited range of tools.

Cons: Although built in a relatively simple way, you'll need to think several stages ahead to make the various components fit. Costly errors may only become noticeable later on. Don't paint the car until you know everything fits correctly. Mechanically, Plus 4s are relatively straightforward, but assembling the wood frame and doing panel work is a great skill. It may be wise to let Morgan experts tackle the more complex areas while you concentrate on other things to help manage/reduce costs. Overall the car will be better for it, and potentially worth more.

Don't cut corners. It's better to have the structure correct and then move on to the more visible items, which can be done over time.

I've seen some fantastic home restorations, and some shocking professional ones.

Take photos and keep every invoice. In ten years' time they will be invaluable proof of the work undertaken.

Ask yourself the 'do you have' questions: Time? Budget? Facilities? Expertise? And the big one: Patience?

14 Paint problems

– bad complexion, including dimples, pimples and bubbles

Cellulose paintwork was the standard finish until 1986, whereupon two-pack paint became standard until water-based was introduced from 1998. The car may have had paintwork repairs, so look for poor preparation and overspray. Look out for the following:

Orange peel

This appears as an uneven paint surface, similar to the appearance of the skin of an orange. The fault is caused by the failure of atomized paint droplets to flow into each other when they hit the surface. It's sometimes possible to rub out the effect with proprietory paint cutting/rubbing compound or very fine grades of abrasive paper. A respray may be necessary in severe cases. Consult a bodywork repairer/paint shop for advice on the particular car.

Cracking

Severe cases are likely to have been caused by too heavy an application of paint (or filler beneath the paint). Also, insufficient stirring of the paint before application can lead to the components being improperly mixed, and cracking can result. Incompatibility with the paint already on the panel can have a similar effect. To rectify the problem it is necessary to rub down to a smooth, sound finish before respraying the area.

Crazing

Sometimes the paint takes on a crazed rather than a cracked appearance when the problems mentioned under 'Cracking' are present. This problem can also be caused by a reaction between the underlying surface and the paint. Paint removal and respraying the problem area is usually the only solution.

Cracking around the headlamp pod.

Corrosion blister. This is on a Superform aluminium wing.

Blistering

Most often caused by corrosion of the metal beneath the paint. Perforation will be found in the metal, and the damage will usually be worse than that suggested by the area of blistering. The metal will have to be repaired before repainting.

Micro blistering

Usually the result of an economy respray where inadequate heating has allowed moisture to settle on the car before spraying. Consult a paint specialist, but usually damaged paint will have to be removed before partial or full respraying. Can also be caused by car covers that don't 'breathe.'

Fading

Some colours, especially reds, are prone to fading if subjected to strong sunlight for long periods without the benefit of polish protection. Sometimes proprietary paint restorers and/or paint cutting/rubbing compounds will retrieve the situation. Often a respray is the only real solution.

Peeling

Often a problem with metallic paintwork when the sealing laquer becomes damaged and begins to peel off. Poorly applied paint may also peel. The remedy is to strip and start again!

Dimples

Dimples in the paintwork are caused by the residue of polish (particularly silicone types) not being removed properly before respraying. Paint removal and repainting is the only solution.

Dents

Small dents are usually easily cured by the 'Dentmaster,' or equivalent process, that sucks or pushes out the dent (as long as the paint surface is still intact). Companies offering dent removal services usually come to your home: consult your phone book/internet.

Micro blistering, commonly found on bonnets and back panels.

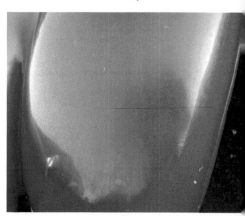

Fading.

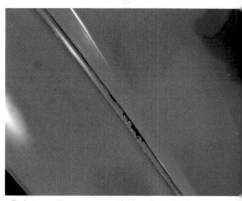

Paint peeling on pre-1986 painted wing beading. The wing is also badly faded.

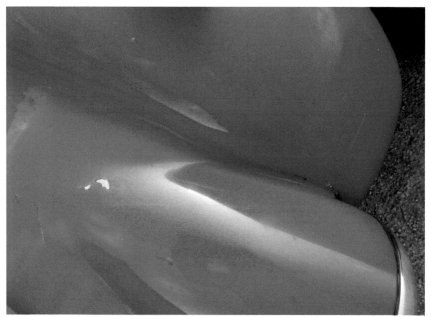
Front wing showing cracking, blistering and fading all within a small area.

15 Problems due to lack of use
– just like their owners, Plus 4s need exercise!

Plus 4s, like humans, need regular exercise to keep them in top condition. Ideally, Plus 4s need a run of about ten miles every couple of weeks as a minimum. Winter storage and periods of very little use can cause problems.

Seized components
Pistons in brake calipers, wheel, slave and master cylinders can all seize. Handbrakes, if left on, whether rod- or cable-operated, can seize (later cable-fitted cars are particularly prone to this). Later AP brake cylinders will seize through lack of use. Brake discs will go rusty and can cause juddering once the car is reused.

The clutch can seize if the friction plate becomes stuck to the flywheel because of corrosion. To free the clutch try pumping the pedal. Running the engine until normal operating temperature is reached, and then trying the pedal may also help.

Post-1993 rear wheel brake cylinders are prone to seizing/leaking if the car is left for long periods. We change lots of these.

T16 ECU mounting position on the bulkhead. Injection relays clearly visible. Relays can stick due to lack of use.

Fluids
Old acidic oil can corrode bearings. Check the colour of the engine oil – light brown is a good sign, black or thick black oil is a concern.

Uninhibited coolant can corrode internal waterways. Lack of antifreeze can cause core plugs to leak and even cracks in the block and cylinder head. Corrosion build up in the system will cause overheating.

Brake and clutch fluids absorb water from the atmosphere and should be renewed every two years. Old fluid with a high water content will cause components to seize and deteriorate. Brake failure can occur when the water turns to vapour as it comes into contact with hot brake components.

Tyres

Tyres that have the weight of the car on them in a single position for a period of time will develop flat spots, resulting in vibration and steering shakes. The tyre walls become hard over time and will crack with age, or can blister (tyre bulges). Tyres should be changed regardless of condition if they are over ten years old.

Suspension

With lack of use dampers can lose their elasticity, or even seize. Suspension bushes dry out, particularly on the rear springs, causing squeaks and groans. Front kingpin bushes can seize causing very little suspension movement and very heavy steering.

Rubber and plastic

Rubber hardens and cracks over time. Coolant hoses and fuel tank filler hoses can perish and leak. Wiper blades harden and split. Plastics can discolour and become brittle.

Electrics

Batteries will be of little use if they have not been charged for many months; conditioners can conceal problems. Earthing and grounding problems are common when connections have corroded, including those inside the car. Any multi-plug connection can corrode and may need cleaning and protection to avoid problems (eg Vaseline or contact spray). Sparkplugs can corrode in an unused engine.

Wiring insulation can harden and fail.

Early dashboard switches become brittle with age and can disintegrate when used. They may need working back and forth to get them to operate if left for long periods. These switches were fitted until 1986.

Digital speedometers lose the mileage reading if the battery voltage drops, if stored in damp conditions, and through lack of use.

Exhausts
Tend to be stainless, but manifolds and catalytic converter flanges can corrode.

Weather equipment
Hoods should be stored fitted to the car, as the material is likely to shrink. Damp conditions will quickly ruin weather equipment.

16 The Community
– key people, organisations and companies in the Plus 4 world

Buying a Morgan is like extending your family. Help and assistance is always on hand, and the social scene is huge. Recommended contact points are:

Morgan Motor Company
www.morgan-motor.co.uk
This is the home of Morgan, where new cars are built. Use the website for more information on new cars, factory tours, accessories, locating used cars, and links to the current dealer network throughout the world.

Morgan Sports Cars Club
www.morgansportscarclub.com
For everything Morgan. Local area groups, club events, quality monthly magazine, and so much more.
Live outside the UK? 47 affiliated clubs are linked with the MSCC. Go to the website to find out more.

Specialist insurance brokers
Morgan Insurance
Tel:01420 594242
www.moginsurance.co.uk

Gott and Wynne
Tel: 01492 870991
www.gottandwynne.co.uk

Heritage Classic Car Insurance
Tel: 0121 248 9229
www.heritagecarinsurance.co.uk

Motorsport specialists
Brands Hatch Morgans www.morgan-cars.com
Richard Thorne Classic Cars www.rtcc.co.uk
Revolutions www.revolutions.uk.com
Techniques www.techniques.uk.com
Williams Morgan www.williamsautomotive.com

Car accessories and upgrade suppliers
Morgan official dealers carry a good range of accessories and upgrades. They may specialise in a particular area or a range of extras for the Plus 4 so take a good look at what is available.

There are a number of independent suppliers who stock a range of vehicle accessories, be it exhausts, valances, dashboards, tuning upgrades, etc.

Librands www.librands.co.uk
Wolf Performance www.wolfperformance.co.uk

Mulfab www.mulfab.co.uk
Sifab www.sifab.co.uk
Belmog www.belmog.com
MK Holztechnik www.mk-holztechnik.de
Heart of England Morgans www.heartofenglandmorgans.co.uk/
New Elms www.newelms.com
Holden Vintage and Classic www.holden.co.uk

For Rover engine parts
Rimmer Brothers www.rimmerbros.com

For Morgan interiors and hoods
Allon White Sports Cars Ltd www.allonwhite.co.uk

Wheels
Motor Wheel Services http://www.mwsint.com

Steering wheels
Moto-Lita Ltd www.moto-lita.co.uk

As I work for at one of the main UK dealers it would be unfair of me to name particular dealers to buy from. To help you decide on a Plus 4, though, I would recommend starting with the car locator on the Morgan website, and then various classic car websites, where you will find some excellent specialists listed.

Current UK main dealers at time of writing
Allon White Sports Cars Ltd www.allonwhite.co.uk
Bell and Colvill www.bellandcolvill.co.uk
Beamish Morgan www.beamishmorgan.com
Berrybrook www.berrybrookmorgan.co.uk
Brands Hatch Morgans www.morgan-cars.com
Krazy Horse www.krazyhorse.co.uk
Ledgerwood www.ledgerwoodmorgan.co.uk
Lifes www.lifesmotors.com/
London Morgan www.londonmorgan.co.uk
Melvyn Rutter www.morgan-motors-cars.com
Oakmere www.oakmeremotorgroup.co.uk
Revolutions www.revolutions.uk.com
Williams Morgan www.williamsautomobiles.com

Useful websites to find a used Morgan Plus 4
There are some other classic car sites, which have the advantage of being updated on a regular basis. Some websites show old stock that may still be marked for sale, so call in advance to ensure a particular car is still available.

These are some of the UK's most popular:

www.carandclassic.co.uk
www.pistonheads.com

www.classiccarsforsale.co.uk
www.autotrader.co.uk

Useful reference books/magazines

Original Morgan John Worrall and Liz Turner ISBN 9780760316443
Making a Morgan Andreas Hensing ISBN 9781787113695
Morgan 100 years Charles Morgan ISBN 9781843172673
MOG magazine Alpha publishing 01905 611926

Note: A workshop manual is not available for any of the Plus 4s. The last manual produced was for Morgan 4/4s up to 1981.
There are various other car and classic car magazines available in most countries, many run special features on Morgans on a regular basis.

Club and dedicated magazines for extra information and events.

17 Vital statistics
– essential data at your fingertips

All Morgans are made at Pickersleigh Road, Malvern Link, Worcester, WR14 2LL.
   Launched in 1950 with a 2.1-litre Standard Vanguard engine, and with a flat-front radiator, the model was developed and finished in 1969 with a TR4A engine. All Plus 4s since reintroduction are fuel-injected (except fir nine Fiat models which had Weber carburettors), and are fitted with five-speed gearboxes.

Fiat Plus 4 1985-1988

Engine capacity	Bhp	Gearbox	Max torque lb-ft
1995cc	122	Fiat 125 special	127

Chassis number starts with an F and four numbers, from F6796-7240. 122 were produced.

Plus 4 Rover M16 1987-1992

Engine capacity	Bhp	Gearbox	Max torque lb-ft
1994cc	138	Rover LT71	131

Chassis number begins with a M and four numbers, from M7569-8666. 357 were built.

Plus 4 Rover T16 1992-1997 (short-door models)

Engine capacity	Bhp	Gearbox	Max torque lb-ft
1994cc	138	Rover LT71, Rover R380 from 1994	136

Chassis number starts with a T and four numbers, from T8549-9597. Model is now built on a Plus 8 chassis. Catalytic converters introduced and compulsory in the UK from August 1992. Stainless steel exhausts standard from 1997.

Plus 4 Rover T16 1998-2000 (long-door models)

Engine capacity	Bhp	Gearbox	Max torque lb-ft
1994cc	134	Rover R380	136

114 changes were made to the car for it to comply with European regulations in 1998. Chassis numbers run from T9574-10856. 17-digit chassis numbers are introduced in 1998, the last five numbers being the car number. Oiler valve system removed in 2000.

Plus 4 Ford Duratec from 2004

Engine capacity	Bhp	Gearbox	Max torque lb-ft
1994cc	145	Ford, Mazda MX5	138
1994cc GDI	154	Mazda MX5	148

Sport models introduced from 2009 do not have a spare wheel nor black wire wheels. Mazda gearbox fitted from 2010. Chassis numbers start with SA94420. Four-seater an option from 2006-2016.

Plus 4 Super Sport 2011-2012

Engine capacity	Bhp	Gearbox	Engine type
1994cc	200	Mazda MX5	Mazda

Launched in 2010. Supplied with throttle bodies, Minilite wheels, rally clocks, early studded hood, in six colours with yellow detailing. Natural wood dashboard. Black leather with perforated detailing. 60 produced. Torque figures have never been given.

Plus 4 Babydoll 2013

Engine capacity	Bhp	Gearbox	Engine type
1994cc	250	Ford	Omex

Available in Kingfisher Blue with white stripes or Westminster Green with yellow stripes. Included limited slip differential, uprated suspension, front and rear disc brakes, four-point race harnesses. 15 produced up to mid-2019.

Plus 4 ARP4 2016

Engine capacity	Bhp	Gearbox	Engine type
1998cc	225	Ford	Cosworth

Five-link independent suspension, unique alloy wheels, red painted chassis, rear centre exit exhaust, trim detailing, LED headlamps, a selection of four gloss and four matt colours. 50 produced.

Plus 4 Club Sport 2018-on

Engine capacity	Bhp	Gearbox
1998cc	180	Mazda MX5

Roll bar, stripped out interior with Tillet race seat, alloy wheels, no spare wheel, track-based model. Torque figure not released.

Plus 4 110 Edition 2019

Engine capacity	Bhp	Gearbox	Max torque lb-ft
1998cc	154	Mazda MX5	148

Initially featuring a number of no-cost extras up to £7500, including: leather colour to choice, Babydoll valance, mohair weather equipment, sports exhaust, and performance seats. Performance and torque as GDI.

Plus 4 Works Edition 2019

Engine capacity	Bhp	Gearbox
1998cc	180	Mazda MX5

Available in Sage Green or Silver, matt painted bonnets with air scoop, back panel aperture and cowl, sports ECU and exhaust, unique detailing. Only 50 produced, Torque figure not released.

More on Morgan from Veloce:

Revealing why Morgan returned to its original 3 wheeler concept after a century.
How the new 3 Wheeler was created, became a best-seller, how it's made. What it's
like to own and drive, strengths, weaknesses and factory improvements made since
the 2011 launch – from modifications, possible developments, and even why it is –
or isn't – your kind of vehicle.

ISBN: 978-1-845847-63-0
Hardback • 25x25cm • 144 pages • 101 colour and b&w pictures

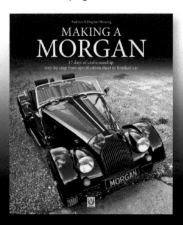

The authors spent seventeen days at the Morgan factory in Pickersleigh Road,
Malvern Link, recording step-by-step – from customer's specification sheet to
finished car – how individual craftsmen handbuild a Morgan. Follow this amazing
journey through the factory, from craftsman to craftsman, by word and picture.

ISBN: 978-1-787113-69-5
Paperback • 27.075x22.8cm • 160 pages • 380 pictures

For more information and price details, visit our website at www.veloce.co.uk
• email: info@veloce.co.uk • Tel: +44(0)1305 260068

The Essential Buyer's Guide™ series ...

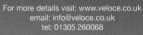

Even more on Morgan from Veloce:

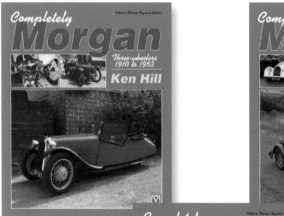

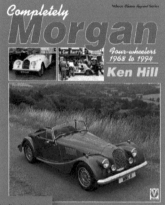

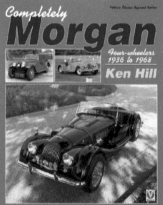

For all owners – and would-be owners – of four- and three-wheeled Morgans, these invaluable books are packed with genuinely useful information.

Index

Auction 69
Automatic gearbox 76
Axle 65

Battery 44, 63
Bodywork 26, 40
Brake system 11, 55, 60, 64, 66, 83
Bulkhead 27, 28, 44
Bumpers 41, 45

Carpets 12, 49
Chassis 29, 44
Clubs 16, 86
Clutch 64, 83
Cooling system 62

Dashboard 31, 49, 50-52
Dimensions 8
Documentation 23, 71

Electrics 12
Engine 34, 89
Exhaust 57, 58, 84

Four-seater 9, 14, 47

Gearbox 44, 64, 89

Handbrake 55
Heater 31
Hoods 32, 33, 36, 47

Immobiliser and keys 53
Instruments and gauges 33, 50, 66
Insurance 10, 86

Kingpins 11, 59

Lighting 11, 43, 45, 61, 76
Long-door 50, 89
Luggage rack 8, 9, 75

Models
    110 Edition 20, 21, 90
    ARP4 19, 21, 90

Babydoll 19, 90
Fiat 17, 89
Ford Duratec 18, 89
Ford GDI 19, 89
Rover M16 17, 89
Rover T16 18, 89
Supersport 19, 90
Works Edition 20, 21, 90
Morgan part costs 11
Moto-Lita steering wheel 49

Narrow-body Plus 4 21

Original Morgan by John Worrall 5, 88

Paintwork 40, 80
Power steering 7

Radiator 11, 37
Restoration 73, 78, 79

Seats 30, 32, 38, 48
Short door 89
Sidescreen 36
Sillboard 30
Specialists 86
Steering 56, 60, 65
Suspension 54, 57, 58, 65, 83

Timing belt 11
Tonneau 32, 47

Underbody 27

Valance 27, 37, 39, 76
Values 17
Vehicle check 23

Weather equipment 12, 32, 36, 47, 84
Wheels and tyres 11, 27, 54, 83
Windscreen 27, 46
Wings 11, 37, 39-43
Woodwork 29, 30, 37, 38, 46

Notes